CONNECTICUT SPEAKS FOR ITSELF

Firsthand Accounts of Life in the Nutmeg State
From Colonial Times to the Present Day

Connecticut Humanities Council

EDITOR

David P. Shuldiner

ASSOCIATE EDITOR

Thomas R. Beardsley

ADVISORS

Jeremy Brecher
Historian, Writer, West Cornwall, CT

Matt Roth
Historian (formerly of Historic Resource Consultants, Hartford, CT)

John Sutherland
Former Director, Institute of Local History
Manchester Community Technical College

Barbara Tucker
Director, Center for Connecticut Studies
Eastern Connecticut State University

Preparation of this book was made possible by funding from the Connecticut Humanities Council to the former Connecticut State Department on Aging, (now the Elderly Services Division of the Department of Social Services). Dr. Shuldiner's position as Humanities Program Coordinator was seeded by a Scholar-in-Residence grant from the Humanities Council in 1984

CONSULTANTS

Robert Asher, History Department, University of Connecticut

Christopher P. Bickford, Director, Connecticut Historical Society

Jeremy Brecher, Scholar in Residence, Connecticut Pubic Broadcasting

Cecelia Bucki, History Department, Fairfield University

Bruce Clouette, Historic Resource Consultants

Karen Cody Cooper, formerly of the Institute for American Indian Studies

Barbara E. Lacey, Department of History and Political Science, Saint Joseph College, Hartford

Ruth Moynihan, History Department, University of Connecticut

Carole Nichols, independent historian

Joyce S. Pendery, independent historian

Trudy Lamb Richmond, Institute for American Indian Studies

Matt Roth, formerly of Historic Resource Consultants

Bruce M. Stave, History Department, University of Connecticut

John Sutherland, Former Director, Institute of Local History,

Manchester Community College

Barbara Tucker, Director, Center for Connecticut Studies,

Eastern Connecticut State University

Tracey Wilson, Brown University

Acknowledgments

Where does one begin? This anthology owes its existence to a large number of lovers of Connecticut and its history. We have listed the advisors and consultants, but so many others have provided invaluable assistance as we pulled this work together. Ommissions are inevitable, so we apologise in advance for oversights. Here goes—thanks to Lisa Broberg Quintana, the Connecticut League of Historical Societies; Amy Trout and Jim Campbell, New Haven Colony Historical Society; Pat Stark, Eastern Connecticut State University; Lloyd Shanley, Harwinton town historian; Bill Kissam, Norwalk Seaport Association; Mary Beth Baker, Connecticut Antiquarian and Landmarks Society; Ralph Bloom, Norwalk Historical Commission; Louise Pittaway, Stonington Historical Society; Sandy Elgee, Milford Historical Society; Lois Calvert, Simsbury Historical Society; Herb Bengston, Manchester Historical Society; Nancy Berlet, Historical Society of Glastonbury; Emily Manning, Connecticut River Museum; Gail Kruppa, Torrington Historical Society, and officers and staff at the Stowe-Day Library, Hartford, the Deep River Historical Society and the North Haven Historical Society. Thanks also to Laurie Atterbury, Donna Dumaine and Cheryl Pokorny at Hall & Bill Printing in Willimantic, Martha Donelin, Fran Funk, Richard Lenzi, Jackson Sumner, and Frank Himmelstein. Our greatest debt, however, is owed to the Connecticut Humanities Council, and in particular Bruce Fraser, Executive Director, and Laurie MacCallum Rayner, Assistant Director for Public Programs. It is their initial inspiration and continued support for the project, "Exploring Connecticut"conducted by the Department on Aging (1989-1993) and the Department of Social Services (1993-1996) that has made possible the preparation and publication of this anthology.

Tom Beardsley
David Shuldiner, May 1996.

CONNECTICUT SPEAKS FOR ITSELF

Firsthand Accounts of Life in the Nutmeg State From Colonial Times to the Present Day

Editor

David P. Shuldiner

Associate Editor

Thomas R. Beardsley

Connecticut Humanities Council

First published in 1996 by the Connecticut Humanities Council,
41 Lawn Avenue, Wesleyan Station, Middletown, Connecticut 06459

Library of Congress Catalog Card Number 95-071071
ISBN 0-910721-00-9

CONTENTS

PART I

IMMIGRANTS, MIGRANTS AND ETHNICS: THE CULTURAL DIVERSITY OF THE YANKEE STATE

PART II

WORKING LIVES: CHANGING OCCUPATIONS IN THE LAND OF STEADY HABITS

PART III

WOMEN'S LIVES: HOLDING UP MORE THAN HALF THE CONNECTICUT SKY

PREFACE

Interpreting Connecticut's Social and Cultural History

This anthology is designed for those readers who want to explore the ways in which the lives of individuals—everyday people for the most part—reflect important themes in the history and cultures of this New England state. The stories presented in these pages are part of what has been called "history from below." That is, they are largely accounts of individuals who have played a part in the social, economic and political development of Connecticut, yet most of them are probably unfamiliar to the average reader. They present firsthand knowledge in the form of passages from diaries, journals, letters, and oral history interviews that, with few exceptions, have never before been published. These are accompanied with historical pictures and photographs, each of which tell a story of its own. You are invited to view these personal statements— both verbal and visual—to develop a deeper sense of the meaning of Connecticut history as actually lived in and witnessed by those who have played a part in defining its unique character and sense of place.

As you explore the selections in this anthology, keep in mind that no accurate account of Connecticut history or culture can be simple or uniform, for the state's residents are far more diverse than the nickname "Connecticut Yankee" implies. Different groups and individuals have had different experiences (personal, social, economic, political, artistic, etc.) that have affected their relationship to the history of the state. And Connecticut—itself a land of immigrants and migrants—has long seen its residents travel to the far corners of the globe, influencing, and in turn being influenced by, developments in industry and the arts in the world at large. The thumbnail sketch below will provide at least a guidepost for this exploration of the "Connecticut experience."

Nobody knows when the first people came to Connecticut, but recent discoveries suggest that it was more then ten thousand years ago. When the first Europeans arrived, the area had long been occupied by indigenous Algonkian-speaking peoples.

These diverse groups made use of a wide range of materials from the local environment, often moving seasonally to take advantage of good hunting, fishing and farming areas. They raised corn and beans—supplemented with fish and game—and gathered plants both for food and medicinal use.

A little over three hundred fifty years ago, English Puritans from the Massachusetts colony pushed into the Connecticut River valley and established the Connecticut colony. They conquered the local Indian tribes, established town and colony governments, and governed themselves according to their religious orthodoxy. Notwithstanding the presence of Indians, African-American slaves, and small numbers of people from other countries, Connecticut life was dominated for the next two hundred years by the descendents of those English settlers, often dubbed "Connecticut Yankees."

The Connecticut Yankees gradually became less concerned with religion and more with individual economic success. When the American colonies declared their independence from England, Connecticut's supplies of livestock and produce gave it the nickname "the provisions state." After the American Revolution, agriculture declined and many migrated out of Connecticut to the Midwest. Meanwhile, manufacturing expanded and Connecticut products were spread by the famous "Yankee peddlers."

Connecticut's booming industries needed workers, and immigrants began to pour from many parts of the world, the largest numbers first from Ireland and Germany, then from Eastern and Southern Europe and Canada. By World War I, two-thirds of Connecticut's people were immigrants or the children of immigrants.

After World War I, immigration was severely restricted for half a century. In the Great Depression of the 1930s, mass unemployment spread across the state. World War II saw another decline in many of the state's manufacturing industries, accompanied by a rapid growth of insurance, finance, education and other sectors of the service economy.

Meanwhile, both jobs and people moved to the suburbs. New groups came into Connecticut cities, the largest numbers being African-Americans from the Southern United States and Puerto Ricans from the U.S. commonwealth in the Caribbean, but also people from many parts of Europe, Asia, and Latin America.

If Connecticut's people have been so diverse, so have the ways in which their experience has been interpreted. This state has often been called "the land of steady habits" by people who valued what they saw as its stability. But it has also gone through radical changes over the years, such as the revolutionary break with England, the shift from a farming to an industrial economy, the repeated modifications in ethnic background, and the change from a rural to an urban to a suburban way of life.

Indeed, Connecticut is a state of great contrasts. While it is one of the most densely populated states, within an hour's drive from the most industrialized urban areas lie dense forests and idyllic lakes. While Connecticut is one of the richest states in the union, it also has two of the ten most disadvantaged cities; the disparity of wealth between the state's capitol city, Hartford, and its suburbs is the third greatest in the country.

It is also a land of surprises. Connecticut's Indians, declared "extinct" on more than one occasion, continue to thrive, albeit in small numbers. Many of the state's residents have, in its history, refused to conform to ethnic and gender stereotypes in work and community life: there have been women working in Waterbury's brass industry; Jewish farmers in Colchester and Lebanon; a lace-making factory in Deep River adapting new technology to an old craft. And finally, the "land of steady habits" has spawned creativity in the most unexpected places. From within the ranks of Connecticut's most "steady" and conservative of institutions—the insurance industry—have come at least two artists who produced some of the most nonconforming (and highly acclaimed) works of their day: the contemporary composer Charles Ives, of Danbury, and the poet Wallace Stevens, of Hartford.

This selection of firsthand accounts is a mere sampling of the great diversity and contrasts of experience that have represented the life of the state. This diversity includes a great deal of overlapping "membership," for all who have more than one identity, based on membership in groups based on gender, age, occupation, religious, politics, and a wide range of special interests. Your relationship to any of these groups will affect your view. You will be a will be a member of some groups, with an insider's view. Other groups will appear alien or unfamiliar. The people whose voices are heard in this anthology speak with a wide range of individual and collective voices, reflecting the complex and changing identities of those who have lived and worked in Connecticut.

PART I

IMMIGRANTS, MIGRANTS AND ETHNICS

INTRODUCTION

Immigrants, Migrants and Ethnics

John F. Sutherland

It has become a cliche by now to say that the United States is "a nation of immigrants." This statement is usually made in reference to the large numbers of Europeans who, while trickling into North America since the 1500s, arrived in streams in the 1800s, and became a torrent by the late nineteenth and early twentieth centuries, until immigration laws in the 1920s restricted their flow. The Native American Indians pre-date all European and later immigrants by several thousand years (see "The First Immigrants" below). And following the Europeans, the United States has been settled by peoples from all over the globe. To make things even more complex, once people arrived, they often moved about considerably, resettling in other parts of the country. Many more returned home after earning a relative small fortune, or failing to earn a living, some simply retraced their steps back to their countries of origin, because of homesickness and incompatibility with the New World.

The land that is now Connecticut was well populated by Algonquin-speaking peoples such as the Mohegans, Pequots and Schagticokes, when the Europeans first arrived. But up until the dawn of the industrial age, Europeans did not appear in Connecticut in great numbers. The first of these settlers were mostly English immigrants who first landed in the Massachusetts colony in the early 1600s, and then migrated overland to the Connecticut Valley. Still, by the early nineteenth century, newcomers did not view Connecticut as an attractive destination. Good farmland was scarce, and opportunities for livelihood appeared to be meager. But with the onset of Connecticut's industrial revolution, immigrants increasingly flocked to workshops, mills and factories in such manufacturing centers as Waterbury, Willimantic, New Britain, Manchester, Middletown, Putnam, Danbury, Bridgeport, Hartford, and New Haven. By 1850, the state's population had increased to 370,000, and thirty-eight thousand of these residents had arrived since 1845.

British immigrants or their descendants dominated the population until mid-century. They farmed or practiced the crafts which they brought from their homeland. Examples are the cutlers from Sheffield, England, who made pocket knives for the Waterville Manufacturing Company of Waterbury. British immigrants such as these have been referred to as "invisible immigrants." They shared the language and many of the customs of the dominant Anglo-American population, and so tended to culturally blend in more readily in their new homeland.

The Irish brought the next major change in the population of the "land of steady habits." Irish immigrants had helped build the Enfield and Farmington canals in the 1820s, but they did not arrive in massive numbers until the devastating potato famine of 1845-1851, during which over a million people were forced to leave the "Emerald Isle." Among these newcomers the men began as manual laborers in such jobs as canal and railroad construction; gradually they joined the factory workforce. Irish immigrant women—sometimes the wives and daughters of these laborers, but often single women who emigrated alone—found employment as domestic servants. It was the Irish who experience the first shock waves of prejudice against the foreign-born in Connecticut.

Many residents of this predominantly Protestant state feared the newcomer's Catholicism. Conservatives resented their widespread enrollment in the Democratic Party. A writer for the *Hartford Courant* complained about "ignorant, degraded and priest-led foreigners." Sometimes violence erupted as when rioters burned Hartford's Church of the Most Holy Trinity in 1853. In 1850, the anti-Catholic Know-Nothing Party succeeded in electing a governor and in dominating the General Assembly. But by the late nineteenth century, the Irish-Americans had become politically powerful, rising to leadership in the Democratic Party and winning election to several mayoralties. They had won grudging toleration. The Irish also served as middlemen or "culture brokers" for subsequent immigrant groups. By 1860, Irish immigrants numbered 55,000. They were more numerous than immigrants from any other nation.

Germans were the other major nationality group to arrive in large numbers before the Civil War. Among their reasons for migration were overpopulation, insufficient land, and the Industrial Revolution's technological displacement. Many were refugees from unsuccessful revolutions in Germany in 1848. Those who came to Connecticut were often skilled workers or proprietors of small commercial establishments. Samuel Colt, the munitions manufacturer, hired willow workers from Potsdam to make willow furniture from the trees that surrounded his factory. Weavers and loom-fixers from Krefeld worked at Manchester's Cheney Silk Mills. German Jews, most of them of the Reform Jewish tradition, settled in Hartford and in New Haven where some started out as peddlers and later came to operate commercial establishments. By 1860, eight thousand German immigrants were living in Connecticut.

In the late nineteenth century, the composition of America's (and Connecticut's) immigrants changed radically. Whereas the earlier arrivals had come primarily from northern and western Europe, those who arrived in the late nineteenth and early twentieth centuries hailed from southern and eastern Europe, particularly from Italy, Russia, and the disintegrating Austro-Hungarian Empire. This so-called "new" immigration transformed Connecticut into the multiethnic state that it is today. By 1910, fifty-five per cent of all the state's immigrants came from southern or eastern Europe.

The Italians came primarily from the Mezzogiorno, or rural, poorer southern Italy. The contadini, or peasants, eked out a precarious existence by farming land for absentee owners. The rise of the American citrus fruit industry reduced the demand for Italian fruits, further damaging the marginal agricultural economy. Thus, Italians departed in great numbers, and many of them came to Connecticut. Often people from the same villages would migrate in "chains" of friends and relatives following one another. For example, natives of Melilli in Sicily settled in Middletown. New Haven and Waterbury were particularly large Italian-American centers, as the newcomers came seeking unskilled and semiskilled jobs in the emerging factory economy. Wherever Italians put down roots, they maintained close-knit neighborhoods of homes, markets, shops and restaurants. Life revolved around the family, the one certain refuge in an uncertain, sometimes hostile world. By 1910, Connecticut's Italian immigrant population numbered 59,954 and was exceeded only by the Irish.

Russia contributed heavily to the new immigration. Most of the new arrivals were Jews. Czarist persecution led some two million Russian, Lithuanian and Polish Jews to migrate to the United States and Canada. Unlike the German Jews who preceded them, they were mainly Yiddish-speaking and less "assimilated," and those who were religious followed the more strict Orthodox traditions. In Hartford, New Haven and elsewhere, eastern European Jews established communities, and sought work as peddlers, grocers, tailors, carpenters and bakers. They founded worker's organizations and mutual aid societies (as did the Italians and other immigrant groups), synagogues and schools (both Hebrew and Yiddish), and organized Yiddish theater groups and choruses. A "Labor Lyceum" in Hartford offered a venue for hearing about and discussing—in Yiddish—the latest cultural and political developments. Smaller Jewish farming communities existed in Colchester, Chesterfield, Norwich and Uncasville. By 1910, 54,121 Russians, most of them Jewish, resided in Connecticut.

The other major group of new immigrants were the Poles. In the nineteenth century Poland was ruled by Russia, Prussia and Austro-Hungary, all of whom tried to suppress Polish nationalism and the Polish language. Furthermore, huge population increases reduced the amount of available land. Thus some three million Poles immigrated to the United States in the late nineteenth and early twentieth centuries. In New Britain they found employment in machinery, hardware and metalwork factories. Poles were often ridiculed as "greenhorns"; for reasons such as this—as well as the cultural isolation faced by non-English speaking immigrants—they formed their own communities. Polish-American life centered around the church. New Britain's Sacred Heart Church is illustrative. Sacred Heart sponsored a school, a religious order, a cemetery, an orphanage, a home for the elderly, a newspaper, and several businesses. Thus it was through the church that Poles, like many other immigrants, were introduced to American life. By 1920, Connecticut contained 46,623 Polish-born residents. Of course, many other eastern European groups—Czechs, Hungarians,

Slovaks, Lithuanians, and others—also settled in Connecticut. Our northern neighbor spawned another late nineteenth century immigrant movement. French Canadians, primarily from Quebec, migrated to the upper mid-west and to New England. In Quebec, as in so many homelands, population growth outstripped the availability of land to support it, and many Quebecois chose life in the burgeoning New England mill towns. In Connecticut they especially moved into the textile towns of the eastern portion of the state. French-Canadian life revolved around family and church. For over two centuries, French language and culture had been an insulator from the unfriendly British-Canadians, and it served the same function in the United States. The French-Canadians established their ethnic parishes, clubs, and parochial schools. Today over 125,000 persons of French-Canadian origin live in Connecticut.

Connecticut's has also provided a new home for many "in-migrants"—citizens who have moved here from another part of our country. Puerto Ricans have been coming to the "mainland" from their Caribbean island home—a U.S. Commonwealth since 1898—since the early 1900s; however, it is only in the period following World War II that they have arrived in great numbers. Employment in the island's sugar, tobacco and coffee plantations is seasonal, and the economy is strained to support its three million inhabitants. Cheap air fare and no migration restrictions have encouraged Puerto Ricans to come to the mainland for seasonal work, and many remain. Originally, they came to work on the tobacco farms, but the decline in the tobacco industry has meant fewer jobs. Most Puerto Ricans in the state live in the cities, especially in Bridgeport, New Haven and Hartford.

Puerto Rican migration has intensified since the 1950s. Hartford's roughly 30,000 Puerto Ricans constitute the state's largest Hispanic community. Most Puerto Ricans are Catholics, with some Protestants—including those who attend one of numerous storefront Pentecostal churches. They have, in recent years, begun to assert their cultural and political strength, forming neighborhood organizations and local lobbying groups to improve life in their adopted state. But their relationship to their homeland remains very close, and the debate about its future status (as Commonwealth or state or independent country) still affects the lives of Connecticut's Puerto Rican residents, who numbered over 88,000 in 1980.

The other major "in-migrants" are African-Americans. They have lived in the state since the colonial era, when they first arrived as slaves; but as late as 1900, they still constituted only 1.7 percent of the state's population. Connecticut passed a gradual emancipation law in 1784, but both slaves and free blacks were treated as inferiors throughout the nineteenth century. Their increased migration into the state began with World War I. Ever since, African-Americans, like immigrants, have come to Connecticut seeking improved occupational opportunities. While Connecticut did not present the legal segregation so common in the South prior to the civil rights movement of the 1950s and '60s, nevertheless informal discrimination did exist. African-Americans created their own churches and social institutions. Housing opportunities were limited, and black migrants moved into inner city neighborhoods from which earlier immigrants had departed. This pattern of creating urban ethnic communities continues for African-Americans as well as other ethnic minorities. The formation of these inner city ghettos and barrios has had mixed results, for while supporting ethnic solidarity, they have experienced disproportionate poverty. Connecticut has become a land of paradox: while boasting the highest per-capita income, it has two of the ten poorest cities in the nation—Hartford and Bridgeport. A recent report of the State Board of Education estimates that nearly eighty percent of the state's minority students are concentrated in 14 of the 169 towns. Some of Connecticut's approximately 217,500 African-Americans have made great gains, but widespread segregation and poverty remain two of the state's greatest challenges as it prepares to enter the twenty-first century.

The latest newcomers are Asians. In 1910, only 462 Chinese and 71 Japanese people resided in the state. But in 1980, close to 19,000 Asians and Pacific Islanders lived in Connecticut. For the first time, the Census Bureau included the Vietnamese as a group, and 1,825 were counted in the state. But the two largest groups are the 4,995 Asian Indians and the 4,691 Chinese. Some are professionals; others are small businessmen, and many are unskilled laborers. Other Asian groups include Koreans, Japanese and Filipinos.

And so, one "steady" characteristic of the "land of steady habits" seems to be that its population continues to change. This phenomenon makes Connecticut, and the nation to which it belongs, a culturally rich and exciting—if challenging—place in which to live.

I

The First Immigrants

Firsthand accounts of the lives of Connecticut's first inhabitants are difficult to come by. The Native American Indian peoples of New England transmitted cultural knowledge through oral tradition. The only existing records are statements attributed to Indians by English colonists who claimed to have written down the words they said. It is difficult to assess the reliability of such documents, but the information they convey has provided some insights into their way of life. The following is an excerpt of an account, supposedly taken down from the words of an unidentified New England Indian by one "A. Holmes." It was among material he donated, in 1804, to the Massachusetts Historical Society, and published in their "Collections." It describes a division of labor between women and men that could be said to characterize most Algonkian-speaking peoples in the region at that time.

As our ancestors had no art of manufacturing any sort of metal, they had no implements of husbandry; therefore were not able to cultivate their lands but little, that of planting skommon or Indian corn, beans and little squashes, which was chiefly left under the management of women and old men, who were incapable of hunting, and little boys. They made use of bone, either moose, bears, or deers' shoulder-place, instead of hoe, to hoe their corn with, tie it fast to one end of a stick or helve made for that purpose. This their way of clearing lands was not so difficult as we should imagine, and that without using an axe. When they find that their fields will fail, they are to prepare another piece of land; in the first place they do, they make a fire round the foot of every tree, as many trees as standing on the ground they intended to clear, until the bark of the tree is burnt through, for trees are killed very easy in this manner. They planted while trees are standing after they have been killed; and as soon as trees are fell, they burnt it of such length that they might roll the logs together, and burnt them up to ashes, thus they do till they get it quite clear. An industrious woman, when great many dry logs are fallen, could burn off as many logs in one day as a smart man can chop in two or three days time with an axe. But the employment of men consisted in hunting and fishing. They used bow and arrow to kill game, with which they were expert. They used to catch deer by ensnaring them with strings. By hunting they supplied themselves with clothing and diet; they seldom felt much want, and they were very well contented with their condition; having food and raiment was their only aim. They were not to kill more than necessary, for

But these English having gotten our land, they with scythes cut down the grass, and with axes fell the trees; their cows and horses eat the grass, and their hogs spoil our clam banks, and we shall all be starved.

there was none to barter with them that would have tempted them to waste their animals, as they did after the Chuckopek or white people came on this island. Consequently game never diminished.

European methods of exploiting natural resources, stemming from a radically different market economy, upset the delicate ecological balance maintained by Connecticut's first inhabitants. To make matters worse, these "new" settlers took advantage of long-standing rivalries among some native tribes who at times sided with the colonists in local conflicts against neighboring Indian communities, rather than uniting with them against this threat to their way of life.

This state of affairs was summed up by Miantonomo, a Narragansett sachem [chief], in 1642. Representing a tribe living in what are now Rhode Island and Massachusetts, he attempted a reconciliation with a rival group of Long Island Indians, led by the sachem Waiandance, who had conspired with the English against the Pequots. Appealing to their common plight, Miantonomo is said to have issued the following statement [his remarks were supposedly recorded by one Lion Gardener, an English engineer; although Miantanomo's exact words may never be known, we may assume that the passage below accurately reflects the important argument he was making]:

Brethren and friends. We are all Indians as the English are, and say brother to one another; so must we be one as they are, otherwise we shall all be gone shortly, for you know our fathers had plenty of deer and skins, our plains were full of deer, as also our woods, and of turkeys, and our coves full of fish and fowl. But these English having gotten our land, they with scythes cut down the grass, and with axes fell the trees; their cows and horses eat the grass, and their hogs spoil our clam banks, and we shall all be starved.

European colonists had very clearly defined concepts of land ownership and utilization, and of buying and selling land as property. Although they recognized well-defined territorial boundaries between groups, Indian people related to land only in terms of usage (the "right" to hunt, gather, and cultivate crops in certain areas), not in terms of real estate. They were often tricked into giving up land utilization rights by Europeans who gained title to the land whose resources they had traditionally exploited. A number of Indians who realized the implications of the new land terms being imposed upon them tried to seek redress through the colonial court system. The following is a petition submitted by a group of Farmington Indians to the Connecticut General Assembly on May 13, 1672.

To the honored General Assembly now sitting in Hartford, the humble petition of the underwritten shows that our selves with some others and our predecessors, having the ancient right to the meadow and upland where the plantation of Farmington now is, being the natives of that place we are fully Satisfied that Some part of the said meadow was by our predecessors confirmed to the English to belong to the English, but other parts of the said meadow, as also the upland to our knowledge, was never either given or sold to the English and is yet not with standing parted amongst them and possessed by them, and we the natives, having often desired to have our land or some good reason why they hold it from us, we can gain neither, and we being now of small power and not willing otherwise to contend do hereby desire the honored court to take our said aggrievance into their serious consideration and to determine it that, in case the true right of the said lands do yet pertain to us, that then we may not be forcibly kept out of our own, and on the contrary, if the English have good title to the said lands, they have hereby an opportunity to clear it up and thereby strengthen it, we have found it hard to have audience from many persons, we desire we may be heard and determined by your selves, which if obtained we shall have ground to believe that there is yet justice to be had from the English, which is all we desire.

May 13th, 1672

Nessahegen his mark X	Kibuckquam his mark X	James his mark X
Tabbhon his mark X	Cherrev his mark X	Qutttamogues his mark X

[Indorsed] Kepequam & other Indians, Petition May 9, 1672.

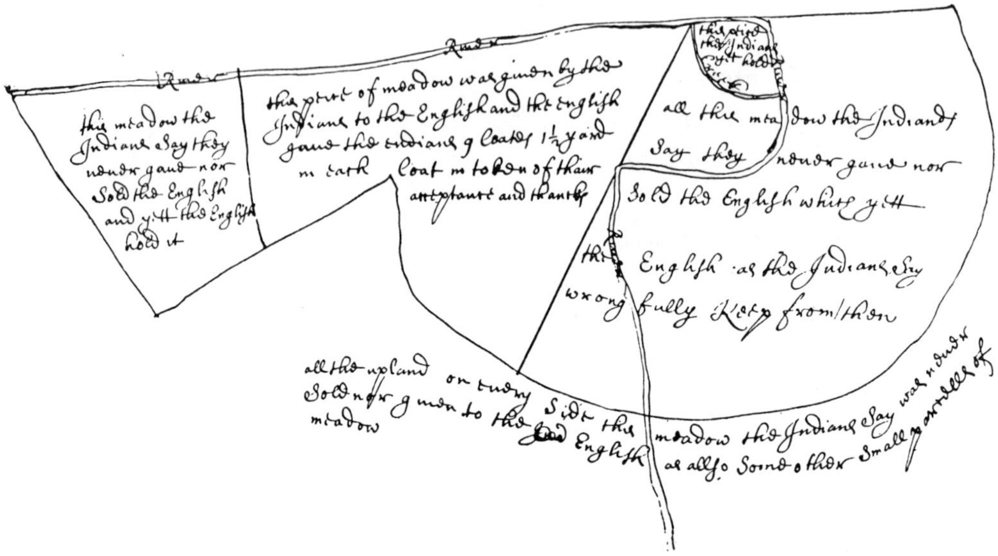

A contemporary 17th century map and description of the meadowland in Farmington, Connecticut, which caused the dispute between the American-Indians and the English.

II

William Grimes

The first Black people to arrive in Connecticut were unwilling immigrants, torn from ancestral homes across the sea, or unwilling migrants, brought up from Southern auction blocks or plantations. African-Americans did not freely migrate in large numbers from the South to the Northeast until the 1900s (beginning in World War I). However, many Blacks who escaped from the bonds of slavery did find refuge in Connecticut in the 1800s. Conditions were not ideal, but certainly a vast improvement. In 1784, Connecticut passed a "gradual emancipation" act, allowing for a slave to be freed at age twenty-five (later twenty-one). In this way, slavery lingered on into the early nineteenth century, but by the 1820s, there were scarcely one hundred slaves in the state. Moreover, those African-Americans who arrived in Connecticut on their own, unless "claimed" by a former master, were considered "freedmen." Many of them had followed the "Underground Railroad," a network of routes to freedom in the north, set up by abolitionists, escaped slaves, and their sympathizers; Farmington, CT, was a well-known "station." Others, like William Grimes, found their own way.

In the introduction to this autobiography, dated "October 1st, 1824," the author offers to those not acquainted with, but who "wish to know who Grimes is, and what is his history, that he is now living in Litchfield, Connecticut, that he is about forty years of age, that he is married to a black woman, and passes for a Negro, though three parts white; that he was born in a place in Virginia, has lived in several different States, and has been owned by ten different masters; that about ten years since, he ran away, and came to Connecticut, where, after six years, he was recognized by some of his former master's friends, taken up, and compelled to purchase his freedom with the sacrifice off of all that he had earned." The following are excerpts from his "narrative," published by him in New Haven in 1855. (Grimes autobiography has been reprinted in Five Black Lives, *ed. by Arna Bontemps [Wesleyan University Press, 1971])*

I was born in the year 1784, in J———, County of King George, Virginia, in a land boasting its freedom, and under a government whose motto is Liberty and Equality. I was yet born a slave. My father,——, was one of the most wealthy planters in Virginia. He had four sons; two by his wife, one, myself, by a slave of Doct. Steward, and another by his own servant maid. In all the Slave States the children follow the condition of their mother; so that, although in fact, the son of ——, I was in law, a bastard and slave, and owed by Doct. Steward.

The overseers have an unlimited control over the slaves on the plantation, and exercise their authority in the most tyrannical manner.

Doct. Steward kept me until I was ten years old. I used to ride behind the carriage to open gates, and hold his horse. He was very fond of me, and always treated me kindly. This made my old mistress, his wife, hate me; and when she caught me in the house, she would beat me until I could hardly stand. Young as I was then, I can yet remember her cruelty with emotions of indignation that almost drove me to curses. She is dead, thank God, and if I ever meet her again, I hope I shall know her.

When I was ten years of age, Col. William Thornton came down from the mountains, in Culpepper County, to buy Negroes, and he came to my master's house, who was his brother-in-law, and seeing me, though me a smart boy. He asked my master what he would take for me; he replied, he thought I was worth l60. Col. Thornton immediately offered l65, and the bargain was made. The next morning I started with him for Culpepper. It grieved me to see my mother's tears at our separation. I was a heart-broken child, although too young to realize the afflictions of a tender mother, who was also a slave, the hopes of freedom for her already lost; but I was compelled to go and leave her. After two days travel on horseback, we arrived at my new master's plantation, which was called Montpelier.

I remained on the plantation about two years, under a black overseer by the name of Voluntine, who punished me repeatedly, to make me perform more labor than the rest of the boys. My master then procured another overseer, a white man, by the name of Coleman Thead; he treated us somewhat better than old Voluntine, but he was very severe, and flogged me severely several times, for almost nothing. The overseers have an unlimited control over the slaves on the plantation, and exercise their authority in the most tyrannical manner.

William Grimes was sold again several times, moving with his masters from Virginia to Maryland to Georgia. He was subject to many more cruelties, and attempted to escape a few times before finally making his way north to freedom as a stowaway on a ship bound from Savannah to New York.

We walked about the city some time; at length, as we were walking up Broadway, who should I see but Mr. Oliver Sturges, of Fairfield, who once had been my master in Savannah. To my great astonishment, he came up to me, and said, why, Theodore, how came you here? I lied to him, and told him I had been there about two weeks; being so frightened, I knew not what to say, never intending to tell a lie, wilfully or maliciously. He asked me how all things were going on at his yard in Savannah. I answered, all well, I just came from there, sir. After a few moments conversation, he passed on one way, and I went on towards my lodgings, where I rested that night. The next morning, after purchasing a loaf of bread and a small piece of meat, I started on foot for New Haven. I could often get an opportunity to ride; sometimes behind the stage, at other, I could sometimes persuade a teamster to take me on for a short distance. In this manner, I arrived at New Haven. After I arrived there, and even before, every carriage or person I saw coming behind me, I fancied were in pursuit of me. Lying still on board the vessel so long, made it fatiguing for me to walk far at a time without stopping to rest; my situation there being quite confined, and no opportunity for exercise.

I often was obliged to go off the road and lie down for some time; and whenever I saw any person coming on, that I suspected, I took that opportunity for a resting spell, and went out of sight until they passed by. Finding my money growing short, I found that I must live prudent. I met a couple of boys on the road who had some apples. I bought them, which, together with what little provision I took with me, was all I had to subsist on until I arrived at New Haven, which was three days. I lodged the two nights I was on the road at private houses.

When I arrived at New Haven, I found that all the money I had left amounted to no more than seventy-five cents. That night I lodged at a boarding house, kept by a certain Mrs. W., who took me to be a white man; and although I have lived in New Haven since that time a number of years, she never knew to this day but that it was a white man that lodged there that night.

The next morning I went to work for Able Lanson, who kept a liberty stable. He set me at work in a ledge of rocks, getting out stone for building. This I found to be the hardest work I had ever done, and began to repent that I had ever come away from Savannah, to this hard cold country.

He set me at work in a ledge of rocks, getting out stone for building. This I found to be the hardest work I had ever done, and began to repent that I had ever come away from Savannah, to this hard cold country.

One day, as I was assisting Isaac (a son of Lanson) to harness a horse, to my great astonishment and surprise, master Stephen Bullock, the relation to and superintendent of my master's office in Savannah, came up to me and said, why, John, it is as hot here as in Savannah (I will here mention, that as it may appear strange for me to have so many names, to those who are not acquainted with the circumstance, that it is a practice among the slave holders, whenever one buys a slave of another, if the name does not suit him, or if he has one of the same name already, he gives him what name he pleases. I, for these reasons, have had three different names). I was so much surprised to see Mr. Bullock, that I could scarce give him an answer. He spoke to me several times. I was so much afraid and astonished, that I could give him no answer. I was afraid he would ask me how I came in New Haven. Who can express my feelings at first seeing him? I behaved so bashful and afraid to speak, that after saying a few words he walked down Church Street, and I saw no more of him. After he had gone, Isaac said to me, why, he appears to know you. I replied, yes, it is no wonder that he knows me. I then went and informed my friends that I had seen my young master, and I did not think it prudent for me to stay in New Haven long.

Accordingly I left town, and went on to a place called Southington, a few miles back in the country, where I went to work on a farm. Here an accident befell me, which I will mention. I one day went to assist Capt. Potter to pick up apples, and having on a red flannel shirt, the cattle were afraid of it as I was attempting to take them from the cart. Having stepped between them, in order to let the tongue of the cart down, which was filled with apples, they started and ran down a hill as fast as they possibly could, I held on to the tongue of the cart as long as I had strength enough. They were constantly kicking me in the face. I durst not attempt to quit my hold, fearing I should be crushed to pieces by the loaded cart; but not being able to hold on any longer, after they had run down the hill, and through a pair of bars, I fell, and the cart passed over me and crushed my ankle severely. The neighbors gathered round me, expecting every moment to see me breathe my last. They took me up and carried me to a house, sent for a doctor, and he came. I being so much bruised and kicked, the blood was streaming from me in many places. The Doctor soon stopped it, and bound up my ankle. I recovered slowly, and was obliged to crawl on my hands and knees a great while, and supported myself on what little money I had acquired, until I procured a pair of crutches. I then used to go around amongst the neighbors in Southington, housing corn, and doing such kind of work as I could do in my situation.

Accordingly I left town, and went on to a place called Southington, a few miles back in the country, where I went to work on a farm.

I found it much harder at this time to be a free man, than I had to be a slave; but finally got to be able to earn fifty cents per day. After I had so far recovered as to be able to walk, or rather limp without crutches, I returned to New Haven. After staying there a short time, I was taken sick, and continued unable to work for a week or two. I put up with Able Lanson, and assisted him in digging a well. I then worked about the Colleges, cutting wood, at which I earned about one dollar a day, of which I was very saving, until I had collected about twenty dollars. I then left New Haven and started for Providence, where I spent the chief part of my money. I then went into partnership with a man by the name of Boham, and kept a barber's shop. After a few months, we dissolved partnership. I then went on to Newport, and after waiting some time for a passage to New Bedford, at length found a packet bound for that part; but the wind blowing very hard, I did not think it safe to go on board, so I put my trunk on board and went on, myself on foot, it being thirty miles, and arrived there before the packet.

I had not money sufficient to pay for my board one week. Wishing to get a place to work as soon as I could, and hearing that Mr. John Howland wanted a servant, I applied to him for employ; we soon struck a bargain at the rate of nine dollars a month; this was in June. In the fall after, I kept shop for myself some part of the time; the rest part I worked for Mr. Howland, until it began to grow cold. I also kept a few groceries. The colored people being often in there evenings and I being a stranger, and the only barber in the place, except white people, they would often come in with their families and dance evenings, until late; and being noisy and riotous, I would endeavor to stop them but no purpose; they still persisted in it, until I was obliged to give up my shop.

I then went directly to Providence, where I remained a few days, then continued on to Norwich, where I went to work for a few weeks, for Mr. Christopher Starr. From thence I went to New London, where I purchased a set of barber's tools. Having been informed previous to this that a barber might do well at Stonington point, after crossing the river I pursued my journey, it being through woods. I had not gone more than one or two miles before I saw four or five men, who made directly towards me. I was very much frightened when I saw them, but could not tell

I had then accumulated about $50, and hearing that there was no barber in Litchfield, (a very pleasant town, about 36 miles back in the country, where the celebrated Law School, under the direction of Tapping Reeve, Esq., was kept), and as there were between 20 and 30 law students, I thought it a good place for me.

why. I was much more so, when they came up to me and said, where are you going, boy? I answered them to Stonington Point. Where did you come from? I came from New London. What have you got there in your bundle? I have got nothing but some barber's tools. You are a barber then, are you? Yes, I was told that Stonington Point was a good place for a barber, and I purchased a set of tools in New London, with the intention of going there to establish a shop. They then replied, there has lately been a store broken open, and we are now on pursuit of the rogues; we have orders to search every person we meet with; we are therefore under the necessity of searching you. I replied, you may search me gentlemen, if you please. They then proceeded to search my bundle, and finding nothing more there than I had told them, let me go on; but advised me not to go there: that the people were not civil, but would raise the devil with any person who should undertake to establish a barber's shop there. They advised me to return back to Mr. Starr's: and after considerable conversation I resolved to return; which I did, and worked on Mr. Starr's farm about two weeks longer. I then went to New London, and took the steamboat for New Haven, where I arrived some time in May.

I then went to work about the Colleges, as I had formerly done; also, shaving, cutting hair, and etc., such as waiting on the scholars in their rooms, and all other kinds of work that I could do when not employed at this. I worked about the Colleges about six or eight months. I had then accumulated about $50, and hearing that there was no barber in Litchfield, (a very pleasant town, about 36 miles back in the country, where the celebrated Law School, under the direction of Tapping Reeve, Esq., was kept), and as there were between 20 and 30 law students, I thought it a good place for me. I accordingly went and established myself as a barber. I very soon had a great deal of custom, amounting to $50 or $60 per month. After I had resided there for about a year with about as good success, I undertook to keep one or two horse and gigs to let. For some time I made money very fast; but at length trading horses a number of times, the horse jockeys would cheat me, and to get restitution I was compelled to sue them. I would sometimes win the case; but the lawyers would alone reap the benefit of it. At other times I lost my case, fiddle and all; besides paying my Attorney.

My acquaintances among the black people were friendly to me in New Haven, and it is no more than just that I should preserve the name of one of them, who is now dead, from oblivion, particularly as he was a runaway slave, like myself and very distinguished in his profession. As soon as I came from New Bedford to New Haven, I went up to College to see Barber Thompson, and to see how he came on; and I found him very sick. He was very glad to see me, and gave the shop into my possession, to keep for him. Barber Thompson, for that was the name he went by in New Haven, was a slave to Mr. Benly, of Port Royal, VA. He came on to the north with a gentleman, to wait on him, and ran away during the last war. He was honest and clever, was called the greatest barber in America, kept shop by the College, and was often called to officiate at parties and weddings, being the politest servant in town. He died last winter, and I had him buried in my burying ground.

That poverty which often leaves my wife and children without a supper, may well excuse me for leaving his grave nameless. A stone I intended to erect with this epitaph:

Here lies old Thompson!
and now he is dead
I think someone should tell his story;
For while men's faces must be shaved,
His name should live in glory.

But I have not for the reason above, put up a stone.

III

Catherine Bond

Charlotte Erikson's Invisible Immigrants (University of Miami Press, 1972), *presents rare correspondence between British immigrant workers in the nineteenth century and their relatives "back home," which captures both the realities of servant life in 19th century Connecticut, and the differences immigrants noted with life in Europe. The following are letters from Catherine Bond—who lived and worked, with her husband James and their children, in Milford, CT— to her brother and a friend in Lancashire between 1870 and 1872. [Spelling has been "modernized" for readability.]*

Milford, Conn., 5 July 1870

MY DEAR BROTHER,

You will think me unkind not to write before now but I shall beg forgiveness and hope you will not be so long in answering mine. It is a splendid country and we all have our health so far. Yesterday was a great day here. It was the day they keep in memory of the proclamation of independence. There was fireworks and guns like we have on the Fifth of November [A British tradition, celebrating the capture and execution of Guy Fawkes, a Catholic, who attempted to blow up the Protestant King and the Houses of Parliament in the 17th century].

The Yankees tell us if there were more English they could send some Irish back.

You wished to know if our master was a Yankee or an Englishman. He is a Yankee, but I think his parents was English. He is a real nice man. If there was plenty like him in England there would not be so many poor people. He is keeping the farmer on this year, for Mr. Fowler was to have sent him a man in January so he did not think it right to turn him away when he had gone so far in his year. But it will be a great expense to him for there is nothing growing on the farm and there is 160 acres of land and 14 cows and two oxen and three horses and about 80 sheep and he will have to buy food for them all winter.

You wish to know how far we are of New York and I should think we are something like being at the Isle of Man from Liverpool. The steam boat comes every other day from New York. I have had a letter from sister Ann. She says we shall be about five hundred miles from where she is. But that is not thought far in this country. How is brother Robert getting on? You did not say anything about him in your letter. Tell him this is the country for them if he gets spliced [English slang for "married"]. The Yankees tell us if there were more English they could send some Irish back. Tell my Father we are a great deal better off than being at Sefton for we have all our wages clear and no expenses.

Your affectionate sister,

C. BOND.

Milford, Conn., 11 October [1870?]

MY DEAR BROTHER.,

Have been kept very busy the last three months. The master has gone back today and Bobby and me has to go to their house in Philadelphia for a week in a fortnight from now. He took the young ladies and me and Bobby for a drive this morning.There is not such scenery in England as there is here. But they don't come up to England in farming. If they did there would not be a country like this. You wished to know if we had any churches here? We have three just over the river, but no Roman Catholic. They will not have any here. I will write as soon as we come back and will send something for father.

Your loving sister,

KATE BOND

Milford, Conn., 1 December 1870

Dear Ellen,

It is not winter here yet, but the Master tells me that it is very severe when it comes. He has given me two pairs of drawers and two woolen stockings for this winter and the Mrs has given me a black scarf shawl for a Christmas present. I had a real nice time of it when I was at the Masters. He took me to the cemetery where his first wife was buried. We was too soon for the train so he took me for a drive in the city. Then he went with me to West Chester 30 miles out of Philadelphia to see a dairy. I stayed there 2 days and then went back to his house. They churn with horse power and the Master has one to churn and cut hay and wood. I went to Church last Sunday for the first time since I was at Aughton. Jim took me across in the boat and bob in his carriage, for J. Berry was in his sulks. He is often in them. I think he will not stop long here. The Master is paying him 25 dollars a month. That is a pound a week and board.

Is the new Church finished yet? It will be Christmas when you get this. I suppose you will be having a gay time of it there. I don't know what sort we shall have here for we have not got acquainted with any one yet. The Yankees are very distant people. They don't think much of John Bulls, but we have lots of mutton and the master said we was to kill a young pig for Christmas. So we don't care much about them.

Affectionately,

KATE BOND

Milford, Conn., 11 July 1872

DEAR BROTHER,

It is haytime and we have a first rate crop, more than the stock will use this year, and they have always had to buy before and there is plenty of fruit, too. But it is so very hot now that the men can hardly stand out to work in the middle of the day. Is father with Martin yet? I often think of him when I see our old gardener here. He has such nice times and gets his 50 dollars a month, and father is working from morning until 9 and 10 at night for a good deal less than that and he is an older man than father and not as good a gardener. But this his last year here. The Master is building a new house for himself. He will be living here next year. He is giving up business. It is a large house built of brick, but he is going to have it painted. But I think it will spoil the looks of it for it is built of patent brick.

Your loving sister,

Kate Bond

Milford, Conn., 22 Dec. 1872

Dear Ellen,

I have not been off the place since the 28th of last month. That was Thanksgiving Day. It is a great day here, as much as Christmas day in England. We went to a friend of ours. They are an English family. There are several here. I will dare say you will think that Jim does not mean coming back to England for a visit, but he has to wait until the workmen have finished in the house.

He is quite disappointed for the thought of having his Christmas in Old England. I don't know when he will start, but I think it will be in two or three weeks at least.

I had a long letter from Peter Taylor last week. He gives a very bad account of the weather and the crops. I am afraid it will be a hard winter for the poor folks. I know it has been a good thing for us coming here. I don't regret it, for we have all we want and are very comfortable. The only regret is that we are so far from our friends, but we must not think to always be with them. We can write to each other, and wherever our lot on earth is cast, we have the same God, and I trust a meeting in Heaven to look forward to where we shall never part. I think that is it that makes me so contented here though I have my children here for company.

From your Affectionate Friend,

C. BOND

Milford Historical Society

Catherine Bond's Milford, c. 1870. Despite Bond's agrarian background, Milford was not particularly known for farming. The community manufactured straw hats and leather goods, and was home to a thriving shipbuilding trade. It gradually became a popular Connecticut destination for vacations after the arrival of the railroads. The Milford churches Bond refers to in her letters are the Congregational First Church of Christ (built 1823), the Plymouth Congregational (1833), and St. Peter's Episcopal (1849). The town's first Catholic church, St. Mary's, was built in the early 1880s. The church visible in the background is the First Church of Christ.

IV

Corrine Hughes

In the 150 years since William Grimes settled in Connecticut, African-American migrants have continued to arrive, each one bearing a story about their efforts to make the Yankee state their home. The story of Corrine Hughes is one. She was born in Jacksonville, Florida, in 1910. Her parents brought her to Hartford, Connecticut in 1912. The varied jobs she held throughout her life represent a catalogue of occupations available to Black women excluded from so many other kinds of work. Through it all, she maintained her dignity and community spirit; after retiring in 1973, she continued to be active in a local neighborhood organization. She was interviewed by David Shuldiner on July 7, 1988, for "An Active Age," a program broadcast on Hartford Community Television.

David Shuldiner: What was it that brought your family to Hartford?

Corrine Hughes: There were a lot of segregationists there, and my father was very uncomfortable with it, so he decided that he better come to Connecticut. He didn't know anybody in Connecticut. There were twelve brothers and sisters in his family and he just picked up and he came. When he got a place for my mother, and there were four of his children, he sent for us, after he got a job. He got a job in the coalyard and he sent for us, and we arrived on Marten Street, in Hartford in the North End. And we lived there until I was twelve, and then he purchased some property in 1924 in Windsor. And I finished school there elementary school—I didn't go to high school. And I went to work. I worked at various jobs like young people do—in tobacco for a while, in the tobacco fields in the summer. Then in the fall, in September up until March, they had a factory where you stemmed tobacco, for cigarettes and cigars. There were different stages—sizing and stemming tobacco. I was doing a little bit of both of them. It was shade-grown tobacco. You had to sew so many pairs of leaves on a lad, and then the boys would take them and hoist them up near the top of the shed. When the shed filled up, they had stoves that they would light, and they would cure the tobacco that way. They would take it to the factory where they stem it—you have to take the stem out—and you had to size it, to size the leaves—they were graded, they had to put them in certain boxes—you would grade the leaves and put them in—they called that sizing.

(The) Asylum Hill Organizing Project...is an umbrella-like organization for many issues...It's older and younger, we help each other when any of us need help, all of us rally together

Corrine Hughes, as she appeared in 1988, being interviewed by David Shuldiner, for the Connecticut Department of Aging sponsored TV series "An Active Age."

Once I was stemming tobacco. That was for the broadleaf tobacco, where they make cigars. You had to get the stems out—they used that for wrapping. And then the other smaller leaves is what they used for cigarettes and whatever else tobacco products. I worked for that in my later teens. And I got a little bit older and I was doing domestic work in Hartford and West Hartford. I lived in and had Thursdays and Sundays off.

DS: Your family still had a house in Windsor?

CH: It was in 1924 that my father purchased his property in Windsor. It was a little farm, about thirteen acres. But then when the Crash hit in '29, nobody could work, and my father lost that property, and he moved back to Hartford. And so we lived in Hartford all that time. Then I growed up and I got married and I got a family—I had three boys and two girls. I got twenty four grandchildren and sixteen great-grands.

In 1951, we purchased our own home. The children—they were in school, and the boys went into the service, and they sent me checks home. We saved up and got enough. Things were cheaper then, in '51, when you bought property, but you didn't have much money. Your salary was very low. At that time. I was working at Aetna Life Insurance—I was an elevator operator there. I worked there for eight years. And then in '51, we moved from Bellevue Square where the kids were raised, to Cleveland Avenue. We lived there for 31 years. It was a three family house. And each one of the children, when they got married, they had a floor, until they got enough together to purchase their own home.

DS: You were one of the many, many women in this country who during the war worked in the defense industry in the factories on the "homefront."

CH: I worked at Pratt & Whitney, in East Hartford. I worked there about three years. During the war, when all the men were gone, they sent me to school, and I learned—I was a machine operator, and I worked on the gears. We had to clean the burr off the gears. It was kind of piece-work like. When the war was over, they laid off a lot of the women. I was a very good worker. But when you stand over me and watch me, I get very nervous.

My supervisor—he was so disgusted when they didn't elect me to stay on, because he said I was one of the best workers there. But this person who was in charge to see who they were going to keep on—he was just standing there and watching me, and I was making all kinds of mistakes. So when I left there, I went to Aetna Life Insurance, and I worked there for eight years.

When I left Aetna I went to the Hartford Board of Education. I was hired as a matron. I had an all-around job. I worked with the kindergarten teachers to help them with the children, getting their things on when they were going home, and when they were coming in, to help them get their things off. And I tidied the room up. Then I made coffee whenever the principals had their meeting there once a month, from all over the city—I knew all the principals. When we started school, we had a party—the teachers would—and I used to make strawberry shortcake for them. I really enjoyed my job very much. And I would help in the office—if they were short in the office, I would operate the telephone—the switchboard, and various things. And then two weeks after school closed the secretary and I had to get all the supplies together, and get them checked in. We worked together for two weeks after school was closed, and we'd come in two weeks before school was open, so we could get the supplies all out, [and] the custodians would take them to the classrooms. But we had to sort them out for each class.

I kept harmony between the teachers and the principal, and mediated between the parents and the children and the teachers. And I would go and call some of the parents and talked with them about whatever was going on, or if there was something the teacher thought that the parents should know, or to get the parents to come in and visit the teachers. I'd go visit the children's parents, 'cause I knew a lot of the parents. This was Mark Twain School. I worked there twenty two years. Sometimes I see the "children" now they are married and got children of their own, got grandchildren themselves. But they always know me, and recognize me. But with them growing up and not seeing them all the time I didn't recognize them sometimes. But they would come over and talk to me. I was working there from 1951 'til 1973.

After I retired, I moved to Shepard Park [a housing project in Hartford for older residents, and for disabled of all ages]. I moved over there, and that's where I got acquainted with AHOP—Asylum Hill Organizing Project. AHOP is an umbrella-like organization for many issues like crime, and for linkage—trying to get developers involved in major construction projects to provide jobs and housing for local residents. I was on most of the boards of directors of committees dealing with those different subjects. They have a parents group, they have a youth group. I chaired several of the meetings we had at City Hall, down at the State Capitol, where all the senior citizens went, some times we had about 500 or 600 people there.

I'm also involved through AHOP with Seniors for Action in Asylum Hill. We go and lobby at City Hall. We worked on getting Medicare improvements, prescription drugs and financial assistance to elderly and disabled for medication, eventually provided for in Connecticut through ConnPACE [CT Pharmaceutical Assistance Contract for Elderly and Disabled], and more coverage for continued hospital care for the elderly, who are often released before they are fully recovered. We keep right after it all the time, we got meetings going on. They were going to close a school—West Middle School in Asylum Hill—and we worked on that with the parents group.

There are a lot of things that come under the sponsorship of AHOP organization. The latest thing we did—there are houses where the landlord wanted to tear some of those buildings down. People wouldn't have any place to live, and if he put those expensive apartments over there, where were the people going to go and live? So they rallied together, and so now AHOP is in charge of the buildings working with a construction firm to renovate them for low-income housing. The people get together and decide what is good, what is best, and we try to get it enforced. It is a very ethnically mixed group of people. It's older and younger, we help each other when any of us need help, all of us rally together.

V

Teresa Sokolowski

Immigrants to this country faced many challenges—overcoming the shock of a new country, adjusting to a foreign culture, finding a livelihood for themselves, and often for other family members. Often immigrants left family behind, sought employment, and earned enough to send ship's tickets for the passage over to remaining relatives. Sometimes friends or relations from the same hometown in the "Old Country" would have already scouted an area in this country where work was available—most often where neighbors, or even employers, spoke their native tongue. Many former farmers found work in shops and factories; some were able eventually to return to the land. The following is an excerpt from the account of a Polish immigrant, Teresa Sokolowski (pseudonym) who settled in New Britain, which still boasts one of the largest Polish communities in Connecticut. She was interviewed by Stan Dabkowski for the WPA Federal Writers' Project, New Britain Office, February 20, 1939 [NOTE: pseudonyms are used where people did not wish to have their name made public or where the source did not indicate.]

I left the old country about forty-two years ago, somewhere about 1898. I remember a good many things almost as clearly as if they happened only a short time ago. It isn't surprising, because hardships and difficulties are not easily forgotten; instead, they always remain in the background, ready to be thought about, contrasted, and best of all elated over because they are forever gone.

And there were certain hardships. You, of course, wouldn't and couldn't understand them as I did, because you are an American, can speak English, and are not a stranger in a strange country. But even if you were, education makes you less of a stranger in any country.

I came to America when I was about seventeen years of age. I came for a number of reasons, but uppermost was the fact that things were hard at home, living difficult on the farm, and I desired to make money in this land about which fancy tales were flowing freely.

There were seven of us in the family, three boys and two girls, and of course, my mother and father. I was the eldest daughter. Our farm was a small one, situated in Russian Poland, far to the west, only about two or three American miles from the German border. It is hard to make a good living when you have only a small farm, with limited animals, and little land to raise crops.

At last we landed in New York after what seemed to me an endless voyage. I felt lost and insignificant, and more lonesome than ever. There were a lot of other people there like myself, and I remember noticing how different we looked from the spectator Americans.

I didn't go away to any school because school was far off in another village. You just couldn't walk all that distance and back just to study, especially when there was so much work to do on the farm and at home. Besides, we had classes in different homes, when sometimes Polish teachers, men and women, would come in from the city and teach us things in Polish and about Polish history. This was on the quiet, of course, for the Russian police were on the lookout for practices of that type, and I remember a few times how we ran when somebody warned us that the Russian police were coming. The church, however, was only a couple of miles away, and we had no trouble going there, or praying how and when we wished.

Then one day we talked about America. My parents thought it would be a good idea if I went there, to make some money, and then eventually to return. You mustn't get the wrong impression about their wishing me to go. You mustn't think that just because your parents wanted you to go that they didn't love you. Oh, no. Underneath, they were thinking of me, and of the entire family's welfare. It is something to contend with when you grow older.

Before I left, I worked over across the border in German Poland; that is, I worked on a farm for a rich family. He had a huge tract of land and many other peasants working for him, but these lived right there on the farm, permanently, in a little home supplied them by the owner. I worked there all summer, and after I concluded, he paid me in one lump sum for all the work I did all summer.

Then fall came, and I was all prepared to leave for this promised land. Everybody cried. They hated to see me go. After all, I wasn't going to any relatives, and I didn't have any letters which would help me once I was here, and I didn't know anything about the language, customs, or anything else for that matter. So they wept, and so did I. They envisioned the various perils I would encounter, and they were deeply concerned. But it was better for all that I go.

I sailed across that huge ocean, and believe me, I was sick all kinds of ways. I don't think you could even imagine how I felt. Young, leaving my land, my people, ignorant, on borrowed money, seasick. Those things mean a lot when you see the shore disappearing in the distance, and for all you know, perhaps for the last time.

At last we landed in New York after what seemed to me an endless voyage. I felt lost and insignificant, and more lonesome than ever. There were a lot of other people there like myself, and I remember noticing how different we looked from the spectator Americans. We went through various immigration formalities under the hand of the officials, and finally I was taken to the St. Joseph's Home in New York, with which Rev. Lawson Bojnowski of New Britain had some supervisory connection.

There the sisters were kind to me. They offered me shelter, as they did to many others. They allowed me to remain for a number of days, and finally secured for me a position in the home of some well-to-do Yankee family. Meanwhile, I had one of the priests of the local parish write letters for me back home, for then I couldn't even write my name. They were all very nice, and it made me feel better.

My education of this new land began once I landed on this soil. Everything was new and different. But how hard it was you'll never know. You can't even imagine it. I just didn't know anything. I was a total stranger. I couldn't speak one word of English. I guess when you can't do that you were considered ignorant, so I think I must have been that. Most of the things I knew I learned in that Yankee household where I worked. I learned to cook, and to speak English. They were patient with me on the whole, and many times it was even funny the way they endeavored to point things out to me in pantomime.

When I went to the store, they always wrote notes for me. I recall the time when they wanted me to go to church. I just didn't know what they meant. They gesticulated all sorts of ways, and I felt silly and hurt standing there like a fool and not understanding. Finally the woman knelt down on the floor and folded her hands as if in prayer, and it dawned on me what she was trying to convey.

Thus, similar things were explained to me. Another time it was raining, and I had to go to the store. I had a large umbrella, and when I got to the door, I didn't know what to do with it, so I

My education of this new land began once I landed on this soil. Everything was new and different. But how hard it was you'll never know. You can't even imagine it. I just didn't know anything. I was a total stranger. I couldn't speak one word of English.

Married life was hard for me...a lot of the young men in those days worked good and hard, and after work, congregated in the different saloons, where they drank and no doubt became intoxicated...They merely wished to be together, to talk, to plan, to recall their mother-country and faraway homes, to mingle with one another in good fellowship.

tried to walk into the establishment just the way it was. I must have looked ridiculous, standing there and fussing with it, and the butcher must have been sorry for me, for he came out and folded it for me, explaining its intricacies to me while doing so. I suppose you couldn't blame us too much for those things. We never had anything like that in the old country.

Some time later, I came to New Britain. A distant relative of mine was living here, and I stayed with him for a while. I boarded like so many others did, and worked in the factory. I labored ten hours a day and received from fifty to seventy-five cents a day for the work. Of course, the prices were a little different from the way they are today, and it wasn't such a large pay, only when you compared it with the old country roubles—then it was a fortune.

In a short time, I was able to send what money I had borrowed back to my family. Then I was married. Marriages were a little different then, too. I mean various other conditions and circumstances had their influence on them. Today, you can court and take your time if you wish to, or wait until you are ready. But not then. We were all young, all lonely, and it was necessary for us to be among our own people. It made you feel better, and closer to home. Getting married was also necessary after a fashion. It had some semblance of security about it in this new land and life. A lot of them (like we) married upon not-too-long acquaintance and with borrowed money.

I remember my wedding. As long as you say no one won't know whom you are talking about, I don't mind mentioning a little about it. I was married in that little wooden church on Orange Street. Just before the ceremony this distant relative of mine with whom I had first boarded tried to have the wedding stopped, on the grounds that I owed him some money (which I did,) and though everything was delayed for some time under the most embarrassing of circumstances, it was finally concluded and I was a wife.

Married life was hard for me. I don't like to talk too much about it, even though I know you, but a lot of the young men in those days worked good and hard, and after work, congregated in the different saloons, where they drank and no doubt became intoxicated. When you think about it rationally, you find that you couldn't blame them too much. They merely wished to be together, to talk, to plan, to recall their mother-country and faraway homes, to mingle with one another in good fellowship.

But marriage isn't always rational. And when you have to run a home under certain conditions, you can deduce without my telling you that it must have been hard. House work wasn't the mechanical and comparatively easy thing as it is today. We had poor facilities, poor light, mostly kerosene lamps, plain furniture, of which most numerous were the beds. This was because I had about five boarders in my home. The men slept in one room and the women in another. There were always as many beds in one room as fitted, and some girls even had to sleep on the floor.

The boarders paid me four dollars a month for staying at my home. I did their washing for them at that price, but they bought their own food, I sometimes throwing in a little soup and the smaller things like salt, pepper, mustard,etc.

My husband worked in the factory, long, hard hours, and I don't mind saying that it sharpened his appetite for drink and also his temper and tongue. I had some good scraps with him, but those I can't be too verbose about. But you just put drink and temper together and you don't have to have me tell you.

In a couple of years I sent a steamship ticket to my sister, and in a few months, she, too, came to New Britain and lived with me. It was good to see her, and to hear news about home and country, even though it was under foreign rule.

Things grew difficult eventually and I did my best to move outside of New Britain, to a little farm. This I did for a number of reasons, the foremost being the fact that I wished to get away from a place where there were so many saloons. So today we have a little farm of our own, a number of full grown children, equipment, and are prospering in a small way.

Today I speak English, am a little shrewder, and am the boss of the family. I have learned through experience that it was necessary for me to do those things. But for me, every time I think of it, as they were then and as they are now—I wouldn't want to leave this farm for anything.

VI

Mr. Frignon

The search for a new home often compelled immigrants to move several times before they finally found a place in which to settle, earn a living, and perhaps raise a family. For many immigrants an important criteria for choosing a location in which to live was the presence of people and institutions to support their ethnic traditions. Mr. Frignon, French-Canadian who eventually settled in Bridgeport, CT, reflects on the road that brought him there, and the problems of keeping French-Canadian culture alive in the face of changing times and conditions. He was interviewed by Vincent Frazzetta, January 2, 1941, for the WPA Federal Writers' Project, Peoples of Connecticut survey. The interviewer attempted to capture a French-Canadian accent in his transcription.

I leave Canada long time 'go and I come to plenty place fore I reach Bridgeport city. I have seen lots of changes from time I leave there to time I come here. Now I am near 63 years old, and I see everything I want to see in this world.

I start to be a farmer, and I finish to be a carpenter

I come from farming people. Far as we remember we are always working on raising and planting, and my people know by nature just how to plant and work with the dirt God gives to them. The old French-Canadian people always have two jobs—if not farming they was working in lumber mills. Some of them go away from their farms, later on, and they go to live where they could find work in the mills. But the old French-Canadians have always the love for planting and living near the ground where they could plant. From the time I was born I always have that feeling—like something tells me that I belong where there is all dirt—planting and raising all the time. But everything is not the same all the time, because I start to be a farmer and I finish to be a carpenter.

I remember my people working all the time on the farm—from when I was small boy to later on, they don't want nothing because if they have enough for living they don't want to look for something else. My grandfather and his people plant to same place for many years, but that time they could live good. When I start to grow big I see that there is not much money to get for all the hard work. My mother and father and everybody in the family have to work from the morning to night, and there is not much to get from all this.

We work here short time because we have an English boss, and he don't like French-Canadian people. Most of the people in this shop was not our kind of people, so the boss makes favors to them and makes everything hard for me and my brothers.

And pretty soon my father is thinking to do something to change—for more money, so the family could live better. That time I was 10 years old, and all the other children in the family was very young. I have to leave school because it is too far to go. So I don't have chance to learn something. And that time all the young children have to help the father and mother with the farm work. I like this, and I don't give much ideas about school because everybody is the same—people too busy—and everybody thinking only about living, and raising the plants. Sometimes we go to the city—few miles away—and we have happy times. French people all the time happy; every place you go you see same thing.

I hear my father and mother thinking about leaving for someplace else, but they never tell the children what they are thinking to do. After I was old enough to understand these things, my father explained to me that there is no more money to work on farm. He said it is better to move someplace where there is use for people that could do factory jobs. He was writing to the uncle in Thompsonville, Connecticut, and this uncle is always telling us to come to live there. He promised to get farm for my father, and he was thinking to get a job for me and my brothers. After this we try to make some ideas about what kind of work we like to do when we move there, but we don't know what to think; we are all farm people and we never think before about learning trades that we could use. Well, after we think over and over we get ideas to work on anything, then if we could learn something else we could see what to do, better. Everybody get excited when we are packing to leave the farm, but we are so sorry to go from the place we are born. We have a hard time to leave, because all the time we are thinking that this place is where all the generations of our people was born.

We come to Thompsonville and we get fixed up right away. My father is loaned enough money to buy a small farm, and me and my brothers find a job in a wood shop. The job was easy, and we have a job to bend the wood that they have to use for making furniture. We work here short time because we have an English boss, and he don't like French-Canadian people. Most of the people in this shop was not our kind of people, so the boss makes favors to them and makes everything hard for me and my brothers. We get laid-off because the boss has different ideas about us; but just the same we understand what the trouble is. He was thinking that we are stranger people and he don't want to trust us. And we can't help this, because all the French-Canadian people that come to the states are all speaking the same. They always stick to the language. From when they are small they do this, and this is something nobody could change. So we get laid-off, and we are trying to get jobs there, but there are no jobs in that city. Next we go to Hazardville and we try to get something to do. Lots of French-Canadian people work there. Pretty soon we come to another wood shop and we get jobs in that place. While I was working here I get the chance to learn the carpenter trade. My brother don't like to learn that so they just keep working on the steady work. I have a good chance to learn, and I think I do good. Next thing I do is go to Worcester, and I find better job there. I was working for a contractor, and he gives me good pay and steady work.

Pretty soon I learned the trade good and I was ready for any kind of work you could give me. By this time my brothers was leaving the shop and they go back to Thompsonville. They want to stay with the family. After I stayed in Worcester I come back, myself, and I get promised of job in Thompsonville. Everything was alright. Soon I get a girl—French-Canadian girl—and she was my religion too. I want her to be that because we are believing it is important to get married with my own kind. By this time my father was selling the farm he has in Canada, and he come back to stay in Thompsonville. What he was getting from the farm was not very much—only to keep him busy. The girls was not working in the shops—they just help around the house. That's the old style we have those time—the girl has to stay home to take care of the housework. The French-Canadians are very careful about their children and they want them to stay home 'till the time they are ready to marry. Now they are different, because the style is always changing.

After I get married I went to Chicopee, Massachusetts and I get a good job there. I was making good money that time, and I was a first class carpenter. I worked on all kinds of jobs, and I made more money than I make in my whole life. We had a baby girl while we lived there, and short time after my wife died and I come back to bury her in Thompsonville. For two years I go to the grave to see her and I was all alone inside. After this I meet a girl through my friend and I tell her to marry me. So we all go to live together in my father's house. We get together good because we are all like one. No fighting like some people have—the French people are all friends with the family. Things go good for long time and then I was hearing about Bridgeport. I find out that Bridgeport has lots of work for mechanics, carpenters and everybody who has trades. I hear that people are coming from all over, just to get the jobs. So I take leave with my family and I come to Bridgeport. I was lucky, because right when I come I find work and I get a flat apartment in the East Side; right near my work in the Remington Company. That time they was building more to the shop and they need men for carpenter work and machine work. I was working for the contractors that have the job; and the job was good. That time was 1915, just before we get in the war. And pretty soon Bridgeport was so busy that it look like New York City. I worked for the Remington for over one year, and then I get jobs in other work in the city. The contractor I work for always kept me busy. All this time I was so busy I don't have time to see other French-Canadian people that live all around me. After, when I have time, I start to go to the organization that they have, and I start to get acquainted with everybody. Many of them, have been going back where they come from, and now we have only those people that have been here for many years.

I worked on construction for many years. Now I am a little too old and I have small repair shop for myself. The business is not so good. And what I make is not enough to make living. But I can't do nothing about this so I stay like I am. My daughter is now married and she has a French husband, and the son is going to St. Anthony's school—that's the school of the church I belong. The school is not so old, it was made by the French-Canadian people, because they are wanting to carry on the French language. At the same time it gives chance to the young people to learn the religion the way we French people have it. This is the same like all the villages the French-Canadians come from. You know one thing about us people? We are all together, and when the French are together they have schools and churches and meeting in their own way. This is something that goes back many years, and a French-Canadian is always the same, no matter that he goes some place else. And the religion follows just the same—here the same like Canada, or anyplace. When I was small my father and mother teach me these things, and when you learn something, when you're small, you always remember this.

When I live on the farm (in Quebec) we work in the summer and spring and autumn, and in the winter time we are making everything out of the wool we get from the animals. That's nice life. In the wintertime we sat in the house and everything is like one family. And nobody thinks about going outside to see better things, because everything in the house is better than you could find. Here we have different kind of life—the girls want to go outside every night, and they have to think about. They meet people from other nationalities and they start to think like these people, and pretty soon they forget they are French people—forget the way the father and mother lived before them.

The French people speak their language all the time. In Bridgeport they do the same like other places where the French come from. French people always use their language in the house, and when they go to church or show or meetings they are using it all the time. This is one thing the French-Canadians never forget; they love to talk the way they have been doing from the day they learn to talk. In the towns and village where we come from everything is done this way. In Massachusetts, in the French sections the people speak one language—French. But this is not the same like the French language from Europe. We are different people. And the French-Canadians keep their language just like the English keep their language when they first come here. So all this time the French talk their language, and this is why they don't speak good English. The French people that come from Europe have different habits like us people. Our people come from there long time ago but in all this time they have changed like different nationalities. Sometimes Frenchmen come to our church and our meetings, but they don't stay long time because they don't understand the way we live—they are different class people.

The French people that come from Europe have different habits like us people. Our people come from there long time ago but in all this time they have changed like different nationalities. Sometimes Frenchmen come to our church and our meetings, but they don't stay long time because they don't understand the way we live—they are different class people.

Parisian French is different language and only people could understand this is people that study real French in the school. But the French-Canadian people have many ways (dialects) to speak and it's awful hard for even French-Canadian to understand other French-Canadian that comes from other place.

Now the French-Canadian people start to separate. Some people move all over the city because they are working in those shops. And people find out they want to live near place they work. So many children don't have chance to go to St. Anthony school to learn the language. The only thing they know is to talk like the mother and father, but to read and write—they know nothing. So I think that in a few years people start to forget that they come from French-Canadian family and they start to be like all the other people. This is not bad, but I like to see French people keep all the good spirit that the French people have for so long.

VII

Emma Reale

Life for many children of immigrants was radically different from that of their parents, as they assimilated more readily into the dominant Anglo-American culture. For others, cultural continuity was maintained as they embraced the outlook and shared traditions of their parents within close-knit ethnic communities. Mrs. Emma Reale, a second-generation Italian living in New Britain, talks about her family history, her views on life, and her sense of ethnic identity. She was interviewed by Doris Matsen for the WPA Federal Writers Project, New Britain Office, sometime between 1940 and 1941.

My mother and father were born in Naples, Italy. My father came from a well-to-do family in Italy and was educated in the English school. His only reason for coming here was in search of adventure, as he had no economic or social difficulties. Upon his arrival in America, he was so impressed by the opportunities here, that after a very short time, he returned to his native land and married his first cousin with the intention of coming back here, and after their marriage, they came back to America to live. The family settled in New Britain, and we live at the extreme end of South Main Street just before Willow Brook Park.

The Italian language was spoken practically all the time. My father spoke very good English, but my mother's English was very poor. Consequently, at home we all spoke the native language of my parents. But when we started to school we spoke the English language and also while playing with the children in the neighborhood.

My father died when my sister, brothers and I were still very young. I was about 11 or 12 at the time. It seems that my father was a great hunter; and while on a trip, he caught blood poisoning. It affected him in such a way that he could only work during the cold months. That meant that mother had to plan her budget so that we could live in the summer even though Dad didn't work.

Well, as I said before, my father left my mother with a family of small children. That is perhaps the reason why my mother had such an influence on us. She always felt that because she was a widow, the neighbors would feel that the children would be left to shift for themselves. This was not the case. In fact, we were brought up more severely than if my father had been alive.

However, I am going a bit ahead of my story. When we children were still young we were allowed a few playmates. But after the age of 10 years or so, my mother refused to let us associate with other children of our age. The reason for this strange practice was due to the fact that my mother felt we would learn too much—more than we should know at our age. I can remember her saying "You learn enough by yourself and you don't need others to teach you any more." Even after I was working at the Parker Shirt Factory on Walnut Street, my mother would not allow me to bring girlfriends home for evening. She felt that I learned enough in the factory during the day as it was. Of course, we were not allowed to use makeup or "prink up" as other American girls of our age.

When my father was alive, he was strict too. We weren't allowed to go to dances except those connected with the church and when either or both parents chaperoned us. In fact, our social activities were centered around the church dances, suppers, family reunions, etc. Of course, we were all taught to go to Mass on Sundays and Holidays. We attended St. Joseph Church and my sister and I went to the different church club meetings.

Oh yes, it is true that the Italians do believe in the Evil Eye, and that it is carried over from the old country. It is quite hard to explain to someone who can't see the result of the Evil Eye, and I can hardly expect to convince you of its power without having seen it for yourself.

I can remember so clearly, an old man living near us who used to come to our house when we were ill and pray over us. After he had said the prayer a few time, believe it or not, we were cured. In fact he was called to my bedside so very much, I could read every word of the prayer on his lips as he said it.

Perhaps it would be better if I stopped and explained just what the Evil Eye means to us. For example, a person who has a headache, backache, etc. is a victim of the Evil Eye. Sicknesses that Doctors have given up as incurable, or unexplainable are also the work of the Evil Eye.

You ask how we know when a person has the Evil Eye. Let me explain—we all know that oil and water do not mix. Take a basin of water and put a drop of oil in it. If the oil spreads out and mixes with the water, the person is said to have the Evil Eye. I firmly believe this because I have seen it done. The procedure is always in threes. The prayer is said in three sections. If the person is not cured the first time, the oil and water act must be performed three times more, and the prayer said each time. Many people, my husband included, thought I was crazy, but they are convinced now. In fact, I have many friends who come to me for help in curing headaches, backaches, etc. You are wondering I suppose just how a person can believe this and still believe in God. The idea is, that all these actions are done in the name of God and with the help of God.

When we lived on South Main Street (New Britain) there were very few Italian families in the vicinity. In fact we often called our neighborhood the league of nations, for there was a German, Irish, French, and Italian family all within a short distance of each other.

But enough for the Evil Eye. To me it is not foolish or unreasonable as some people think, but I do not intend to convince any one of its power. Both my parents were firm believers in the Evil Eye and I guess their influence was strong enough to last.

The Italian language was spoken practically all the time. My father spoke very good English, but my mother's English was very poor. Consequently, at home we all spoke the native language of my parents. But when we started to school we spoke the English language and also while playing with the children in the neighborhood. When my father was alive, he tutored my sister in the Italian language, just as it was taught in the schools (she was 13 years old when he died). I have often wished that I had had the same opportunity as she did. My daughter is now taking Latin in school and intends to make that her vocation.

As I said, before going to school, the Italian language was spoken with greater fluency at home than the English language. However, it is almost impossible to associate with American children and not learn the language. So, when I started to school, I could speak both languages well enough to converse fluently. When I entered school I felt just as any American child entering for the first time—not handicapped in the least.

When we lived on South Main Street there were very few Italian families in the vicinity. In fact we often called our neighborhood the league of nations, for there was a German, Irish, French, and Italian family all within a short distance of each other. The German family lived across the way from us. From them we learned many German expressions. There was one expression I remember so clearly: when the children wanted to come across the street to our house, they would say in German, "We are going across the street." The expression "Iber de Strasse" means across the way, and I can still remember it. We used to say "Mother, we are going "Iber de Strasse". There were many sayings that we said at the time, but I have since forgotten them. We also learned to eat molasses and bread and tomato jelly from that German family. At the French home, dances were held and we were allowed to attend. I remember one boy in that family who could not speak English to any great extent. One type of food that they ate and which we children did not like, were acorns. They ate them with relish, but we children couldn't swallow them. Then there was an Irish family close by. They had two or three children our age and we used to play with them most of the time.

When I was old enough, I went to the Northend School on Bassett Street. Miss Sheldon was my teacher in first or second grade. I thought a great deal of her. In fact, I think she was my first ideal—one to whom I looked up. At Christmas time I took part in the Christmas play. Miss Sheldon made my costume and I was as proud as a peacock. I can see it now—it was a red-checked dress with lots of ruffles. It's funny how certain things stay with you. I can even remember a few lines of the piece I said:

> "No, no, said he with a laugh of fun
> I'll have no cheating my pretty one."

The idea of the play was that I had put up two stockings for Santa to fill and he knew there was only one little girl in the house.

No, I can't say as there was very much discrimination against the pupils and teachers. I suppose this was because there were so few of each nationality—not enough to form groups or clubs of their own as they do today.

When St. Joseph's School started, I was changed from the Northend school to the Catholic school. I was only there a very short time when I was changed back to the Northend School again. It seems that after my father took sick, and was only able to work in the winter, we were unable to pay as much as we ought to. For this reason there was a feeling of antagonism against me as well as my family. In fact, there was a noticeable discrimination. That was the reason I was changed. I merely finished grammar school and then was forced to go to work.

I have always been made to understand that I must respect and love the Italian flag as well as the American. I guess the fact that I had so much respect for my parents led me to love the flag of their native country. Anyway, when the Italian flag is displayed, a feeling of true love and allegiance comes over me—something I have no control over. My parents did influence us and taught us to respect the Italian flag and Italy, but they never for a moment forgot that American was our native land. They never kept us from paying our respects to America, and its government. From early childhood, I have seen pictures of Italy and heard my parents tell me of their life in the old country. Is it any wonder that I feel for my parents' homeland?

Between the ages of 15 and 20, I often rebelled against the idea of my not being allowed to do things that other girls did, for instance, having girlfriends come home for an evening, makeup, public dances, etc. but I have been very glad I was brought up that way. In fact, my own children are unable to see it now, but I know that they will see differently when they are my age.

My son came to me the other day, and said to me, "Mother, don't you think you are a bit old fashioned?" I was practically taken off my feet at such a question. I just smiled and said, "Yes, I am old-fashioned but that was the way I was brought up by my parents and I'm sure you wouldn't want me any other way."

I have always joined both the Italian clubs and the American clubs as well. However, I have never been hurt or discriminated against to my knowledge. My sisters and brothers are apt to feel and act more American than I, by joining clubs, associating more with Americans than Italians, etc. I feel that I can be of more use to the Italian people than to the Americans because I can understand their ways.

From early childhood, I have seen pictures of Italy and heard my parents tell me of their life in the old country. Is it any wonder that I feel for my parents' homeland?

I have always felt at home both with the Italians and the Americans. However, I think the fact that my husband who was born in Italy, and came to this country when he was twenty-one would have some bearing on the situation. We both belong to

Italian clubs. Perhaps you have noticed that my husband does not speak very good English. The reason for this is, that his father and mother in the old country, were dependent upon him, and he felt obliged to send them the money that he would use to get an education. Furthermore, he had no time to spend for education, as it was necessary for him to begin immediately to make a living.

I do not identify myself as an American only. How could I? I feel that I belong to two groups or rather that I am a happy medium between each—American and Italian. I respect both nations equally.

As I said before, my relatives have become more Americanized. They don't exactly feel ashamed of their nationality, but they consider themselves as purely Americans. While I am an American citizen, I still feel as though I should help rather than discriminate against my own descent.

VIII

Irma Johnson Harrison

In striving to settle in and adjust to life in their adopted home, many immigrants gradually found themselves relying less on traditional cultural institutions as they negotiated their way through the world of industry and commerce. (This was probably just as true for those rural peoples who migrated to urban centers in their countries of origin.) They and their children often didn't realize the degree to which they had assimilated until they tried to recall the customs no longer practiced in their families and communities. Irma Johnson Harrison, a second generation Swede whose family settled in Manchester, CT, talks about her family history, and a lost cultural legacy, still maintained by her parents, but not passed on to the next generation. She was interviewed by John Sutherland, Director of the Institute of Local History, Manchester Community College, on June 20, 1980, who opened the interview by asking about Swedish immigration into Manchester, Connecticut.

I have been told, but I didn't know too much about it at the time, that my grandparents came over. My grandfather's mother came with them—that would be my great grandmother. They settled on Chestnut St. My mother was their only daughter. She was about twelve years old when they came here. My grandfather was a tailor and had a little shop downstairs where he did tailoring. My mother went to the schools here in Manchester. My grandmother was a hard worker and lots of these Swedish immigrants would come over and they would come to their home; eventually they would find work for them at Cheney Brothers [silk mill]. As far as church goes, they walked to Hartford to go to church—there were no Lutheran churches in Manchester. Eventually they would meet around the different homes and a student or someone came in as a substitute preacher. In 1881 they organized the first Emmanuel Lutheran Swedish church. There were twenty original members. My mother was organist there for twenty-one years. This year we're celebrating our 100th anniversary.

Mother always served Swedish foods, Swedish dishes of all kinds. We do a lot of that even today. We have *korv*, which is Swedish baloney. We make *dreeko* which is root beer, which was always a tradition in our family, and bake Swedish cookies and coffee breads.

My father's father had a farm in Sweden. He went to school in Sweden, to agricultural school, and worked on the farm. And when he got to be eighteen, his mother died and his father remarried—this was not a happy home for him, so he decided to come to the U.S. He got into New York and had about $28 in his pocket, and decided that wouldn't take him to Minnesota, so he came to Manchester. He went to work at Cheney, for two and a half years; his health failed at that time. He got a job down at Teachers Hall. He did dishes, worked in the kitchen, etcetera.

The Harrison Family

Irma Johnson Harrison, and her husband, Albert , pictured together in the mid-1980s.

There was a Jane Cheney that lived there at that time. He used to bring water up to her in the evening, whatever she needed. This went on for about a year, and one day she called him up to her room, and she asked him who he was working for and what his ambitions were. He talked with her for a long time and things went on for a while. She called him back and she told him "My brother, William Cheney (who owned the Cheney store) would like to talk with you, and I think you would have a job down there." My father said, "I'm perfectly happy doing what I am doing." She said, "Well, I think you could better yourself." He went to work at Cheney store in the basement, sweeping, etcetera. Finally, he worked up to the main floor, and Mr. Cheney was very good to him and increased his pay every once in a while. Then Father decided that it was time he had his own business, and that's when he decided to go into the grocery business over here at grandmother Magnell's, in the basement. He would go out in the morning, call on all the different customers and get their orders, then he would go back and fill them and deliver them in the afternoon. After a while his business grew and outgrew the basement. And that's when he decided to build the Chestnut Street store. He was very successful there. He had about six clerks working for him. At that time they had the wagons and the horses. We children—there were five sisters, five daughters and one son, and at Christmas time he needed extra help. We would go over and package their coffee and sugar and do up the groceries, which was a lot of fun for us. He had a candy counter, but he always said that the candy counter belonged to the children. They used to come after school with their pennies. That's the only reason he kept the candy counter. The store was very popular with Manchester's Swedish people. My father sold Swedish rye flour, and the kyrum seed—all those things that go into making Swedish things. He catered to them.

I was born across the street at 62 Linden. When my parents were first married, all this land through here was virgin land. He evidently bought this lot over here and that's when he built that house and that was at the turn of the century. Grandmother Magnell's house was here. My two older sisters were born on Eldridge Street. They were four and five years old when they moved up here.

The rest of us were all born over here, but we continued many Swedish traditions. At Christmas time we had Joullata at church. That was our 5:30 a.m. service. The family all came home and they would put cots up in the third story, the house was full of people. We all got up at 5:00 in the morning and went to church. That was quite a thrill. Mother always served Swedish foods, Swedish dishes of all kinds. We do a lot of that even today. We have *korv*, which is Swedish baloney. We make *dreeko* which is root beer, which was always a tradition in our family, and bake Swedish cookies and coffee breads.

We always had Christmas fairs at church—we always contributed homemade things for that. For many years we had a Swedish bake sale at church. They don't do that anymore. People don't like to bake anymore. I'm not one of them, but anyway, we used to have Swedish bake sales, they were very popular. The food didn't last very long. Once in a while we'd have a craft fair and bring in all kinds of Swedish artifacts. It's really interesting

Manchester Historical Society

The Park Hill Grocery on Chestnut Street, Manchester, pictured in the early 1920s. This photograph was probably used as a promotional piece. It features the owners and staff, and the store's horse drawn and mechanized delivery teams. Irma's father obviously found a niche in the market, serving and catering to Manchester's Swedish population.

to see what people do have. There are many Swedish families in town now, the descendants of the original Swedes, so many of them talk Swedish, if they have someone to talk with. I can understand, I can talk some.

When I was confirmed in church, we were confirmed in Swedish. I didn't understand a word I was talking about but, I learned my catechism by heart. That was when Pastor Cornell was there but soon after when the next minister came, the Swedish language was discontinued. Now with our anniversary we are going to have Joullata this year and we're going to have Pastor Foster Gustafson, do you remember him at all? Probably it was before your time. He's coming and will preach in Swedish. We'll have a real Swedish festive time for our anniversary.

My family spoke English and Swedish mixed. We understood, we could understand my mother and father. My grandfather talked mostly Swedish. When I was that age, I could understand and speak it but you get away from it and forget. I also learned some Swedish in the Sunday school because I didn't have it in school at all. Now that I am older, I wish they had pursued it further because I wish I knew now a lot more about it than I do.

IX

Lucy Addy Richardson

Many immigrants brought experiences and skills learned and practiced in the land of their birth—and they found similar employment in their adopted community. One of these was Lucy Addy Richardson, formerly of Portadown, Northern Ireland (Ulster), and long time resident of Manchester, CT, when she was interviewed on June 5, 1980, by John Sutherland for Manchester Community College's Institute of Local History Oral History Project. The interview has been edited into a continuous narrative.

I was born in Northern Ireland in a little village called Bann Foot. There was a little street with ten houses on each side. That was in the middle of the countryside. There was a pump right in the middle of that street, right beside my home, and the public house was right there. I was born right beside the public house and that was away at the end of the world as I thought as a child. Living there with the Bann river on one side and Loch Neagh at the other side, it seemed that I was surrounded. I was away from everything, and that was the end of the world to me. I remember this anyway.

In our Manchester neighborhood, a lot of the people came from Bann Foot or the surrounding villages. It really was Irish. One third, or maybe half, was Irish.

My mother was a hand-loom weaver, but at that time my father was a handyman around the countryside. He did a lot of different types of things; for instance, he would roof the houses, the thatched roofs. You have to be someone that understands just how to build those things. For the schoolmaster he would do odd jobs. He would work in the field—in the moss where the turf was cut. That's peat, you would call it here. It was what we used in the fire, of course, we had the hearth fires and we didn't have coal or anything like that.

We had a linen weave shop, we called it, built onto our home. It was big enough for four of these looms. They are quite a large thing and they have a treadle. We had two looms there at that time, after I was born. My sister was ten years older, and she was a weaver and my mother was a weaver. But me being little, I was about five, and I remember winding the bobbins to keep my sister going with her loom. My mother was provided with the bobbins, and I didn't have to worry about her. Sometimes now I think of it, I was just a child, and I really rebelled, and sometimes I wouldn't have the bobbins in time. My sister would holler for

Manchester Historical Society

The "millgirl" featured above is not the subject of the interview, but nevertheless this c. 1915 photograph shows a typical, unidentified spinner at work— who may well be Irish—in the Cheney silk spinning mill, replete with the long skirt and raised hair of which Richardson speaks.

the bobbins, and I'd bring her a hat. So that really was my life at that time. Of course, I was going to school at that time. We started school at three years old in Bann Foot. Well my life was happy: I didn't know anything different. There wasn't anything much to do.

Most of the people in Bann Foot were weavers. But there were farmhouses around the surrounding countryside, they had the land, they owned it, they were more affluent than we were then. My father would work for them at times, and then my mother of course stayed home, but she wove, and she did practically everything for those children: she had nine during the period. I understand when she had her first child, her first children, there wasn't even a safety pin or anything like that, and they had to put straight pins in their babies' diapers. So it was really primitive.

My father came to America alone. He came to one of his cousins. In that time, he came over and then he lived with my cousin in Manchester. Families would keep boarders. That's the way they lived. They would have about half a dozen boarders from the old country, and then those boarders would help them with clearing up the meal table and doing lots of things in the house. But anyway, my father went and lived there with one of those cousins. He worked in Cheney's, as far as I know, a velvet weaver. Then, he sent for one boy and again he sent for another and then. But during the interlude he went over home, back to the old country to see his family, and he brought some of the boys with him coming back. That was three boys and my father were here. Then they planned to bring others; we still had six people to come. So this is all surmising, I never thought much about it. At the time I didn't realize the responsibility of these things. So we got a boat; it was the *Campania*. It was its last trip, it was so old. My father, with the boys, they had saved enough money, and they rented a home here for us to come. When we got here, we had a home. So we came over on the boat. I was sick most of the time, between seasickness and toothache, I don't remember too much about it. We came second class. That meant that we didn't have to go down in steerage. Steerage was where you stayed there, and you didn't get up on deck. It was really a terrible thing, and we used to look down at all those people, and see them and realize that we might have been down there. So finally we came over here. It took us a week. During that crossing, that was the time in 1914, when the *Lusitania* was sunk and Britain started to fight.

One of my brothers, the oldest brother, met us in New York. He had been here first. He had to herd us through the traffic and everything—oh, that poor man! One of my brothers, I'll always remember it, he almost got run over right in the middle of the street and Billy saved him. I'll always remember that. That was the day or the time when we got the cold milk. I had never tasted cold milk in my life. Cooled by the refrigeration—we didn't have any of that. We never did. And it was quite something to do that, to taste the milk. Then we came on the train. I had never been on a train before.

In our Manchester neighborhood, a lot of the people came from Bann Foot or the surrounding villages. It really was Irish—one third, or maybe half, was Irish. There was lots of Italians at that time too. Then I got in with a lot of girls my own age. I started to get used to the place. In Portadown we had belonged to the Salvation Army, and when we came here, that's what we belonged to. I had a brother and a sister, they were ministers in the Salvation Army. Then, of course, my [son] Robert, he was a Salvationist, he played, he's a musician.

The Polish, Lithuanians, and Italians, lived mainly in the north end of town. There was another thing: there was caste there. We were supposed to be in a better district. They were looked down upon, then. It was really too bad; I didn't realize it then, in my young day, but I do now. They came over on the train, and if you said you lived over North, you were looked down. It's different today. It's all built up. They took Cheney's Goat [South Manchester Railroad]: We walked. (See Page 72)

In those days, many people took in boarders to supplement the family income. We took in one girl. We really vouched for her, and she lived with us for a while. That's the only one. Where we put her, I don't remember. We had all those of our own, and where did we...? Oh, I don't know! We had two in a bed, and two beds in the room, so you would have four in the room. That's why we had to get a bigger home on Newman Street. That was better; we had another bedroom. These other people who had boarders, they would have about four of their own, anyway. They would take in the boarders, because they had to live, and they had to have enough food, and then had a monster table, and the cooking...it was really a job. No, we had enough of our own to take care of.

The landlady that my father had, she said, "you know, you're gonna have to put your hair up: you'll have to get a long skirt, because they won't give you a job." So finally I went, and I got the job. And weaving, imagine, and silk weaving is entirely different to linen, that I was used to. Oh, I hated that job! And I really didn't care whether I worked or not. I was only young, seventeen, and I had girlfriends and, sometimes we'd go to the ladies room, and we stayed there for a half hour or so. I always remember, sometimes I would leave my loom going, and when I'd come back there would be something damaged in the web, and it would have to all be ripped out again, and oh! I got scolded for that. I hated the weaving! Finally I didn't want to work at the weaving anymore. It was hard to be shifted from one job to the other. I didn't seem to be very well. I was having trouble at the time with my system. I got a job over in the spinning mill, the Clock Mill.

I started as a doffer. A doffer had a container that he wheeled around, and when this spinning frame was finished—when the bobbins were finished—then the doffer would come and take all those off, and put them in this container. As he took the full one off, he put an empty one, until he would go along the frame. There must have been about twenty or thirty bobbins on there that he would take off, maybe fifty on that big frame.

Then I stayed at that for quite a while, and finally graduated to a spinner and I like that pretty well. Before I was married, I wanted to change my job again, the spinning was quite heavy. I went into the doubling. The doubler, you would put two spools—it was in another building—two spools of thread, and then you had a contraption that would double those together. So I learned that, and I stayed on that until I got married.

Life was different when we came here. Portadown was kind of a little tiny city. It had a main thoroughfare, and it had bigger buildings and churches all around. The houses were all joined.

When we came here, it just seemed like all country, all meadows, and houses were not joined together. There weren't many sidewalks. We didn't have as much chance to visit with the people. In the old country, on Saturday nights, everybody went out. There was a big main street in our place, and everybody went out and walked up and down, and met everybody else and had the most wonderful time. There was nothing to do really. In Manchester, it was different.

We really had to rearrange our lives all together. But eventually we got used to it. See, the houses were different, they were wooden and they looked different. We did have better facilities in the Manchester house. In Ireland, we didn't have any indoor toilets or anything. But here it was different. One thing was strange: the stoves were heating systems. We had fireplaces in our rooms downstairs in Portadown. We had them in the living room and dining room; sometimes they would have them in the bedrooms. Here we had just the stove, the black stove, and it seemed the strangest thing I had ever seen. Of course, we got used to it. And I suppose the other things would be different too, if we went back. At first, I was homesick, terribly homesick. We were terribly homesick, because it was as if we didn't have anybody. America was entirely different, of course, to what we had been used to. But after a while we got used to it.

Below: This aerial view of the Cheney silk and velvet mill complex in Manchester, Connecticut was taken during the late 1950s. The older weaving mills, where Lucy started work, are located in the top left hand corner. The picture also reveals the dyehouse, yarn mill, velvet mill, printing department and, in the top right hand corner, the doffing and spinning mills where Lucy eventually worked. For more information on the Cheney silk mills, refer to William E. Buckley's *A New England Pattern The History of Manchester, CT* (Pequot Press, 1973).

Manchester Historical Society

Manchester Historical Society

Lucy Addy Richardson refers to *Cheney's Goat.* It is pictured above, c. 1900, at the old Cheneyville passenger station. *Cheney's Goat* was a 27 ton Baldwin tank-type, coal-burning steam locomotive. It was purchased by the Cheney company in 1884 as a passenger and freight transport engine.

Cheney's Goat traveled some 16,000 miles a year without leaving Manchester. It was in service until 1935, and was sold to the Case Paper Mill in East Hartford. It was scrapped in 1949.

The 2. 25 mile South Manchester Railroad (SMRR) on which *Cheney's Goat* worked, was completed in 1869. It connected the Cheney silk mill complex with the Hartford, Providence and Fishkill Railroad depot in North Manchester, and was initially designed to transport materiel rather than passengers. The SMRR was expanded and modified in the early 1880s. Rolling stock was purchased to provide transport to the mills for the growing section of immigrant workers residing in North Manchester, such as the Polish, Lithuanians, and Italians refered to by Richardson in her interview.

Passenger service on the SMRR ended in 1933, and freight services were taken over by the New York, New Haven and Hartford Railroad, the Penn Central Railroad, and finally by Conrail.

X

Mr. Moses

Not all Connecticut Yankees shared the anti-"foreigner" sentiment expressed by young Raymond Blair, (pp. 87-88). "Mr. Moses, Age 75, three (grown) children," was of a very different mind. He was likely a descendent, not of the founding fathers of Connecticut, but of the laborers or skilled workers who came from England, and made their contribution to the growth of the state along with all of those anonymous immigrants and children of immigrants who preceded as well as followed them, leaving their marks in the products of their labors and the memories of family and friends. "Mr. Moses" is notable for his openness towards other ethnic immigrants, recognizing the importance of their contributions to the growth and character of the "Yankee" state. He was interviewed by Francis Donovan in Thomaston, CT, for the WPA Federal Writers' Project, Ethnic Studies Interviews, in 1939.

Yes, it's a rather unusual name, but it's Yankee none the less. The family came to this country from England long before the Revolution, according to family tradition. We never were much for genealogies and family organizations, and that sort of things. As for the Moses part of it, my father was a deeply religious man, and a great student of the Bible and Moses was one of his favorites.

The fusion of races has always produced a sounder, healthier, more energetic people. I'm all for it. If people would just put aside their prejudices and hatreds, and realize that we're all Americans in the last analysis, bound by common interests.

I suppose if I hadn't lived my life in a small town where everybody knows everybody else, I'd have often been mistaken for a Jew. That's what the boys in the shop used to tell me, anyway. With that black curly hair, and that name, you'd pass for Jewish anywhere. Well, the hair isn't so black, and it isn't so curly any more.

I worked in the shop here nearly fifty years. Retired ten years ago. After my wife died, you see, my daughter and her husband offered to come here and keep house for me. I wasn't feeling so well at the time, and there was no real reason why I had to keep on working, so I quit. I was a toolmaker. Education? Why, I like to think of myself as self-educated. I read a great deal. Since the time I learned to read I've never been without books. They were hard to get, when I was young, too, but I managed to get 'em. My father encouraged me in it, because he was kind of a bookish man himself. I read at least two a week, and there are countless old favorites that I've read and reread. About this time of the year, I always like to read Dickens. I don't think any other author ever captured the spirit of Christmas the way he did. I don't care much for the radio, no. There's so much of it that really isn't worth listening to. And so much that's repetitious. I suppose they can't help it, they have such a tremendous demand for material.

I'm getting a bit too old to go out much. I see an occasional movie, if it appeals to me. I intend going next week to see *Drums Along the Mohawk* because I read the book and liked it. But nights I rarely leave the house. I never did care for going out, for that matter, and neither did my wife. She was a reader, too. Yes, I go to church regularly, but I don't belong to any of the church groups. As I said, my father was a very religious man, and he impressed upon me the importance of a father in a man's life. And he used to say, "The trouble with the world is there's too much religion and not enough Christianity." He believed in going to church, but he also believed in reading his Bible and practicing what he read seven days a week instead of one.

I'm not registered with any party, and never was. I've never missed voting in a national election, but I've always voted the ticket that looked best to me after careful study. I believe more people have done exactly that in recent years than ever before, and it's a very good thing for the country. The state of the rest of the world during the past few months has made Americans conscious of their civic duties, too, and I'd be willing to bet there'll be a record vote in 1940. And I hope so. We've got a wonderful country here, and a fine, upstanding freedom-loving people, and we want to preserve the status.

No, no, no, that's exactly what I don't believe. I think the character of our people was improved by immigration and assimilation. The fusion of races has always produced a sounder, healthier, more energetic people. I'm all for it. If people would just put aside their prejudices and hatreds, and realize that we're all Americans in the last analysis, bound by common interests. They're getting a broader viewpoint, year by year. You don't hear the expressions "Wop," and "Polack" and Hunky" nearly so often any more.

There was a lot of that sort of thing in the shop, years ago. Just plain ignorance, and medieval prejudice was the cause of it. The Yankee workers thought themselves superior to immigrants of whatever nationality. They never lost a chance to rub it in.

I can remember, during the panic, there was a woman named MacIntosh, a widow, not long over from Scotland, who had a cleaning job over at the old movement shop. It only brought her a few dollars a week, and she worked hard for it, and Lord knows she needed it, for she had three children. She was allowed to continue working even though the place was closed down, because they kept a kind of skeleton crew to keep things in order. But finally Edson Thomas, the superintendent, said he wasn't going to let "that foreigner" keep her job when there were Americans out of work. So he fired her. But his father Aaron Thomas, the president of the company, heard of it, and he put her right back on the payroll. Aaron was way ahead of his time, in that respect. I mean there were probably a good many more people in town with Edson's viewpoint than with Aaron. There may be today, if a count was taken. But I'm optimistic enough to doubt it.

XI

Rachel Himmelstein

Immigrant groups still tend to be regarded as culturally homogeneous. But experience for members of any given group is actually far from uniform. This is certainly true for those Jewish immigrants who came to Connecticut between 1880 and 1930. In the course of their settlement they took up a wide variety of occupations and lifestyles, from garment workers in New Haven to business and professional people in the Hartford area to farmers in Colchester, Lebanon and Montville. A brief portrait of one such immigrant follows.

Rachel Himmelstein, 91, left Russia in 1900 at age five with her parents, initially settling in New York. At the time, the Baron de Hirsch Fund (a Jewish aid organization established by Baron Maurice de Hirsch, a wealthy Munich banker and financier) was offering loans to Jewish families to resettle in agricultural areas in Connecticut and elsewhere. Rachel's parents took advantage of this offer, and bought a dairy farm in Lebanon. Rachel talks about her early life on the farm. She was interviewed in her home in Colchester, CT, on February 14, 1986, by John Sutherland. The interview has been edited to read as a continuous narrative.

I was born in Russia, May 15, 1895. My parents left Russia for economic reasons. There was a better future in America and they had some relatives who had already come here. Somebody paved the way for them and later they paved the way for others. We arrived in New York City, and lived there for a couple of years, I think. My father was in charge of some building—an apartment house. He took care of it. I think it was in Market Street, New York.

I started school in Lebanon. There was a one room school house that my sisters and I went to. Then later when I was ready for high school we came to Bacon Academy in Colchester.

Later, some friends of my father had bought a farm in Connecticut and they urged my parents to come out to Connecticut and settle there—buy a farm and be people in Connecticut. My father had worked on a farm in Russia. So he left New York and bought a farm in Connecticut, in Lebanon. He had saved up the money from what he was doing when he came to New York and took out a mortgage from the Baron de Hirsch Fund which everybody did in those days. I was about seven or eight years old at the time because I went to school in Lebanon.

The Lebanon farm was about 100 acres. It had cows and chickens and a couple of horses and my parents raised their own vegetables. We had one large farm house and there were, of

Frank Himmelstein

Rachel Himmelstein, aged 20 poses in the Willimantic studios of photographer, Laurence Berry in 1915, after graduating from the Willimantic State Normal School (Teacher Training College). Rachel had previously graduated from the Bacon Academy, Colchester in 1911. She went on to teach in Lebanon (1915-1920), Colchester (1920-1924), East Lyme(1924-25), Marlborough (1925-26), and Colchester (1926-1960).

Rachel officially retired in 1960, but returned full-time to work at the Colchester Elementary School to co-ordinate a reading program. She also taught adult classes in Colchester to help people attain American citizenship. Rachel eventually retired in 1978, aged 83, after a 63 year-long teaching career in eastern Connecticut.

course, a barn, cow barn and chicken coop. We had an ice house, we had our own ice for the summer. We had fruits, vegetables, raised corn. We had that for the animals and for the winter. My father marketed the produce. Markets in those days were not what they are now. He sold some eggs once in a while. There was a milk company who took our milk and had it in big cans. We had our own milk cows.

During the summers we used to have what they called "summer boarders" in those days. Women with their children generally came out and they stayed for several months sometimes. We rented rooms and fed them. There must have been about twenty boarders at times, and they would stay the whole summer. They came mostly from New York. It was like a hotel. The boarders ate in the dining room—we had a large dining room. My mother did all the cooking. Later when we had larger groups coming out, she used to get a cook for the summer. But there was plenty of work for the family, just to keep the place going. My sisters used to do the cooking, too.

I had three sisters and two brothers. We had to feed the chickens. Wash things, utensils from the milking and so forth. We did a number of things. We were not idle. We did whatever we could, whatever we were able to do. We all chipped in.

On the farm, we spoke two languages. My parents, generally, talked Jewish [Yiddish] because they did not learn the English language as well as we did. We talked in English to each other mostly and my parents talked Jewish. They spoke Russian and Polish and other dialects similar. I started school in Lebanon. There was a one room school house that my sisters and I went to. Then later when I was ready for high school we came to Bacon Academy in Colchester. I then went to what they called a Normal School in those days—a teachers college now—in New Haven. It's called Southern Connecticut College now [Rachel's first job was teaching in the same one-room school in Lebanon where her formal education began; she later taught at a country school in Colchester, where she, a sister, and eventually her parents moved.]

My family practiced an orthodox Jewish religion, and we kept a strictly kosher house. But there was no local synagogue, and the farmers used to meet on a central farm. The farmers would give them a room to pray in and later, in Lebanon, the one room school was not being used any more and the farmers got that to hold their services in. All of the farmers were well versed in Hebrew and took turns in conducting the services. Someone who was better fitted for it would be the leader.

Our family kept together as a family and paid no mind to differences in generation. We were still the same people, despite the problems of adapting to a new culture.

Frank Himmelstein

Above is the homestead/farmhouse in Lebanon described by Rachel Himmelstein. It was located on Route 16 on the Lebanon-Colchester line, but burnt down in the 1970s. The picture was taken in 1910, but unfortunately the people featured in the photograph have not been identified. Rachel Himmelstein was 15 at the time, and may be one of the two girls in white dresses at bottom left. The man and boys in the buggy may be Rachel's father and brothers, and the people on the porch could include Rachel's mother and sisters, and summer boarders.

XIII

Alex Lopez

The experience of Puerto Rican "in-migrants," and the development of the Puerto Rican community in Waterbury is strikingly similar to that recalled by other immigrant groups. [Puerto Ricans in the U.S. are unique in that they are both immigrants in the sense of coming from a distinct Caribbean island culture, yet technically migrants because their Commonwealth status makes them U.S. citizens.] The following are excerpts from an interview with Alex Lopez, Waterbury resident, conducted by community historian Jeremy Brecher on July 8, 1981.

I came to this country on August 6, 1950. I came to New York. My godfather's stepbrother was there. He sent me up to Connecticut, because there used to be some Puerto Ricans working here who would go back and forth every weekend. He figured I'm better off, because in New York I might have gotten lost. In those days in New York, anybody working in the hotels or something like that made maybe thirty-five dollars a week. It was good money then, but you had to wake up at 3 o'clock in the morning to get to the job at 6 o'clock. I came down with these guys who worked at the foundry. They lived in Naugatuck, in a boardinghouse. On South Main. It's not there anymore because they built the highway. It used to be a nice place.

It is very hard to come into another culture. Some people work their way into the American people more easily. For Puerto Ricans it's hard.

When I came, everything was strange for me. I didn't speak any English at all. There were about fifteen Puerto Ricans living in that boarding house. These friends of mine took me to the foundry. They gave me a job. It was nothing like I expected. It was with a shovel. The sand comes in on the wagons, and you've got to shovel out by hand. I had a tough time in there. They had a guy, he was like a little supervisor; if the boss went away, he'd take over.

The boardinghouse was cheap in those days. You only paid ten dollars for a room. I got my lunch. The lady was nice. Treated us good. She was not Puerto Rican. In those days there was nobody with any position like that. In those days I remember only one Puerto Rican who had a wife and kid living in an apartment. The lady who kept the boardinghouse was Italian. A nice lady; she gave a good meal for that kind of money. Sometimes we had to share the room, maybe three beds. That part wasn't bad because we understood each other; there was nobody else in there besides Puerto Ricans. Some worked days; some worked nights. The ones who worked days couldn't sleep because the ones who worked nights came down in the middle of the night.

Later on some of the guys went to New York and bought some rum. On the weekend they'd go crazy. The place took a name: They called it La Casa del Diablo because of the noise. After I got out of the house, a Puerto Rican took over.

The main problem for us Puerto Ricans was that there was nobody to communicate with. Usually we like to joke around, we like to talk; one talks, another listens. That's why, when you go around, you see a bunch hanging around. They want to talk, laugh, joke. We like that. We'd do that in the beginning, but the policemen used to come around and say, "Break it up, break it up, break it up." Without reason. We noticed they'd only break up the Puerto Ricans' group. But we couldn't say much.

Some new guys came into the boardinghouse and started working in the foundry. These guys became my close friends. We'd go out together to the bar, hand around. So we made a very close friendship. They told me, "Why don't we get a little apartment someplace?" We went to Union City and found a nice apartment with four rooms on the third floor. We lived better out there, because there was nobody else.

This guy told me: "My mother is going to come from Puerto Rico. I want you to go meet her. She's going to come to New York." I said O.K. But he didn't tell me that he had a sister. I went to see his mother and I saw that girl over there. "Who's she?" "Oh, she's my sister." That's my wife today. I started to go to New York, because I met the girl who is now my wife. Every weekend I'd go back and forth. I came in 1950 and was married in 1953. I worked in the foundry. If anybody is going to look for a job in some other place, they had to know good English. I wanted to get out of there because I didn't see any improvement. I kept working with the shovel. Another fellow and I quit, because somebody came up and said, "What are you doing there? Why don't you come to work at Megin Construction?" That was a big company in Naugatuck "We're making around $1.65 an hour out there." We only made about $1.35 in the foundry. So we quit.After that I lived around different places.

We went to work for Megin and we made a few more pennies. But it started to get cold. For him, winter was a new experience. Some guys told us, "You've got to be careful; it might be too cold." They started to scare us. So we sent a notice to Mr. Jensen, who used to be the personnel in the foundry. He wanted us to work there because we did a lot of work. If he would put us inside, we would come back. We were afraid to be outside. He said, "Yes, come down; we've got something for you." The other guy got a job grinding, so he made more money. But me, he needed a man to cut the sand. About the same job, only inside. The worst part was you had to start at nine o'clock to get off at eight o'clock.

There was a Pole doing that job with me. When all my friends would go around 3 o'clock, I couldn't talk to the guy. The guy didn't know English. So I hated that part from three o'clock until we finished. To stay there with a man and not talk to each other, like we were mad. I put in a year like that.

The main problem for us Puerto Ricans was that there was nobody to communicate with. Usually we like to joke around, we like to talk; one talks, another listens...We'd do that in the beginning, but the policemen used to come around and say, "Break it up, break it up, break it up." Without reason.

I told them, "I want to make more." The boss didn't want to take me out of there because that job was the kind of job nobody wanted to do. It was very hard to get somebody in there. So he played games with me. Like one time he said, "Yes, I'm going to make you a molder, but you have to wait." They never put me in there. So I decided to quit. But I worked one-and-a-half years before I quit.

You can see what happens to somebody who doesn't speak the language. I wanted to be independent. In the beginning I had no choice. But I didn't want somebody always to have to help. So I started to pick up here and there a little English, so I could defend myself. One day I wanted to go home because I didn't feel good. There was a guy who used to be an interpreter for everybody. He said, "You want me to tell the boss?" I said, "I'll tell him." I went to the boss and said, "Me sick you; go home." He understood; he laughed. He made a joke out of it after that.

After I met this girl, my friend decided to bring his mother down here. He got an apartment in Waterbury. His sister, who is my wife today, came too. So I decided to move up here to Waterbury. I found a room on Meadow Street. I considered these people family already. Her mother reminded me of my mother. We got closer and closer; before I knew it, I had a family.

I started to work in Scovill's [brass mill] August 11, 1953. I worked two and a half years in there. I started working on the second shift. What I was doing was not like in the foundry, but I didn't know how to do anything, I didn't learn anything in that place. So I was a floorman; he assists somebody who brings the work to the guys, the operators.

About fourteen months later I got married. We got married at Our Lady of Lourdes. I decided to stay at Scovill because I got good benefits, insurance. I didn't want to jump around. I've been in that place twenty-eight years now.

Before they passed the civil rights law [Civil Rights Act of 1965], they didn't hire many Puerto Ricans [for 10 years, he was the only Puerto Rican working at Scovill]. After that, they started hiring Puerto Ricans. They're not many problems with discrimination because if we see anything like that happen, with the union we put it through right away. There's always something cooking, but the union is always there. If anything looks like discrimination, right away we put in a grievance.

In the beginning we had a lot of problems. It is very hard to come into another culture. Some people work their way into the American people more easily. For Puerto Ricans it's hard. Puerto Ricans have been here thirty years now, since 1950. If we're here another hundred years, we're still going to speak Spanish, and we're going to keep on doing the same things we do in Puerto Rico. That's the way we are. A very small amount of the ones born over here go to American ways of living. Our kids speak Spanish; they eat what we eat; they do things like we do.
In the beginning people didn't understand the Puerto Ricans. But now they get in there. Got not choice. If you see something every day, all of a sudden, even if you don't like it, you start to get to feel comfortable. I see American people now are getting to be much better with Puerto Ricans. After all, we Puerto Ricans like to spend a dollar.

It is very hard to come into another culture. Some people work their way into the American people more easily. For Puerto Ricans it's hard. Puerto Ricans have been here thirty years now, since 1950. If we're here another hundred years, we're still going to speak Spanish, and we're going to keep on doing the same things we do in Puerto Rico.

The main organization that we are associated with is the church. Almost everybody, directly or indirectly. It's a place for everybody. Besides that, we've got a club; we've been working since 1958. We've got a place up on Baldwin Street. It's an old place we bought there. It's very hard to get good members.

We've got a book full, but there's only about thirty-five who are working to keep the place. It's a social club. We get together sometimes. We celebrate family parties. We have little dances. We make some money to keep up with expenses, with the mortgage. It's almost paid now. The whole idea of this club is for everybody, for the future. Maybe somebody, my children, will have something. We say that, but most of the people don't understand that, don't believe that. It's a tendency of Puerto Ricans here to say, "I'm going back to Puerto Rico next year."

Another thing you didn't ask me, but I'm going to tell you: People don't want to go out and vote. We should have a big political power here, "Political muscle" they call it. We don't have it. We should have at least 10,000 voters. We might have 500. It's hard to get into people's minds the idea of the system in this country. Which is no different from our country, because we have the same system. Out there everybody votes. Here, I don't know what's the matter. We tried to put it across.

XIII

Raymond Blair

"Raymond Blair, New Haven, 28, Single, Clerk," represented a view widely shared by many Connecticut Yankees in the early decades of the century who felt threatened by more recent arrivals to this country. Claiming "seniority" through his colonial ancestors (notwithstanding the fact that Native American Indians preceded them by over 10,000 years), he bemoans the social ills of his day, laying blame on the doorstep of those later immigrants who he thinks have damaged the solid foundation laid down by his Scottish forebears. He was interviewed by John P. Kilgore for the WPA Federal Writers Project in 1940.

The ancestors of my mother and father came from the north of England and I think there was a bit of Scotch blood in both families. They came to this country about the same time. I think it was about 1720. The Blairs settled in Massachusetts and my mother's people, the Champions, went to Minnesota about 1730. They later returned to Boston. My great grandfather settled in Connecticut and we have lived here ever since. We have all been Americans in every sense of the word. I was early taught that the old time American stock was superior to all other races and I think it is today. I found that many of the boys and girls with whom I grew up and went to school with didn't seem to give much thought to such things. They took for granted that they were above other races but did not try to find out why. I think their parents were to blame for not giving them information about such things.

I want you to know how a real American feels about his country.

Of course other races have helped develop this country but you can't ignore the fact that the foundation of those ideals and laws which has made this country greater than any other were laid down by pioneer Americans—descendants of English, Scotch and Irish.

My family were not wealthy but we had a good home and my father and mother taught us that there were other things in the world besides money. I graduated from high school and went to work. I am studying now in my spare time to become a construction engineer.

I was taught to keep informed of what was going on in the world and I read a great deal. I don't belong to any societies or clubs. I like outdoor life and enjoy more than anything else tramping the woods and sailing a boat.

I think the Jews and Italians professing to be 100% Americans is bunk. They are not. They are always thinking and talking about their home countries and it would be a better America if they were all sent back. This was a white man's country in the beginning and should be kept so.

I suppose I am pretty dumb about some things but I cannot understand why any man or woman should find fault with American principles, which give to everyone deserving them a chance to live and work in peace and security. Of course, lack of intelligence is responsible for much of our national unrest—but a big mass of people are swayed and led by these dirty, vicious and selfish leaders of various groups who are in turn under the control of foreign governments. Their whole aim is to destroy existing conditions of freedom and decency and they are all looking for personal economic security without contributing their share toward securing it.

I don't want to believe that such horrible conditions as exist in Europe today will ever exist here. The very large majority of the people all wish to live in security—stop fighting and work out their own problems. Why is it so hard to get this country to prepare itself against aggression? My own idea is that rotten politics are responsible for a great deal of our trouble. Respectable, honorable men won't go into politics,—they can't be successful politicians and keep their self respect.

Members of those races which have settled in America during the past fifty years, I mean the Jews, Wops, Polocks and other unprincipled breeds have but one idea—get rich, no matter how, and pay no attention to our laws. They have cost us untold millions for their criminal acts and obstruct the normal growth of our country.

I shall do all I can during my life to fight off the rats who are tearing down the wonderful structure built by our ancestors. Every real American who is white should do the same. There is no need for me to say anymore. I think you have gathered from my talk how I feel about the points you brought up. I am glad to have you know how a real American feels about his country.

PART II

WORKING LIVES: CHANGING OCCUPATIONS IN THE LAND OF STEADY HABITS

INTRODUCTION

Working Lives: Changing Occupations in the Land of Steady Habits

Jeremy Brecher

Few aspects of Connecticut life are more universal—or more varied—than work. Whether old families or immigrants, rich or poor, urban, suburban or rural, almost all of Connecticut's people have made some contribution to its history through their work. And they have left their mark in countless ways, for few places in the world have been host to the sheer variety of occupations as this state.

Until 1800, most of Connecticut's families grew their own food, made their own clothes, and met most of their other economic needs themselves. This self-sufficiency had been well established by the first inhabitants—those Native American Indians who had long settled in the area they called Quonotikut, "Land of the Great Tidal River." European settlers learned much from them, and brought with them their own tools and survival skills. Men and women divided the work, with each requiring an enormous range of skills, from weaving to canning and from carpentry to horticulture. Skilled crafts people such as millers, shoemakers and blacksmiths made most of the other products used in Connecticut's farm villages.

But gradually Connecticut's towns began specializing in industrial products they could sell. The first woolen mill opened in Hartford in 1788. Danbury produced 20,000 hats in 1800. By 1850, Connecticut had the highest manufacturing output per capita in the country, and more people worked in industry than agriculture.

The market for Connecticut products was initially created by the famous "Yankee peddlers" who carried "Yankee notions" to the frontier farming regions of the South and West. Most of the burgeoning Connecticut industry was at first based on handicraft skills, supplemented but not replaced by machines. Sometimes machine production itself required skilled industrial craftworkers.

But after the Civil War, more and more Connecticut production was centered in large factories. Labor in the new factories was far different from the previous farm and handicraft work. Large numbers of workers were concentrated in each workplace; their activity was closely supervised by the employers; much of the work was taken over by machines; most jobs were subdivided into small, specialized tasks which required little skill and which would be repeated over and over by the same worker.

Connecticut industry became tremendously diversified, producing such products as phonographs, ammunition, hardware, brass, bronze, rubber, typewriters, electrical and machine shop products, silk, cotton, woolen goods, hats, corsets, apparel, paper, bread, and many other consumer products.

By the 1920s, barely five percent of Connecticut's population lived on farms. More than half the working population were in manufacturing—nearly two-thirds of them making metal and cloth products. In World War I, Connecticut produced more than half of the nation's munitions. Although insurance, banking and commerce were important in the state's economy, less than 15 percent of the working population were in clerical occupations or trades.

After the middle of the twentieth century, industrial jobs began to decrease; many of the state's most famous companies began closing factories: Dictaphone, Scovil, Uniroyal, Gant, Armstrong Rubber, International Silver, Torrington Company, Robert Shaw, Bridgeport Brass, Fuller Brush, Royal Typewriter, and Singer Sewing Machine, to name a few.

Meanwhile, there has been a steady increase in nonindustrial jobs in insurance, education, health, and other service fields. The typical Connecticut worker today is more likely to work in a service occupation than in manufacturing.

Work has come to mean different meanings to different people. For some it is simply a source of income; for some, a source of dignity, pride and challenge; for others a tedious—and perhaps health-threatening experience.

The experience of work has also been different for different groups. Men and women have generally been channeled into very different jobs. Blacks, Puerto Ricans, and many other ethnic groups have been discriminated in the workplace.

Work is closely connected with the family. A prime motivation for work is to contribute to supporting a family. Often more than one family member in Connecticut has worked and helped support the family. Of course, women have long had primary responsibility for performing housework—the usually unpaid labor of maintaining the family household and providing for the personal needs of its members (often in addition to work for wages for the family income).

Work has also shaped community life in Connecticut. The location of jobs has largely determined where people can live. A history of Bridgeport, for example, noted that the city's industries "are grouped along the railroad lines east, west and north, and the housing of wage earners follows in the same directions, and along the bus lines" (from a W.P.A. history of Bridgeport). Some Connecticut towns, like Thomaston and Manchester, were originally "company towns," in which housing and services as well as jobs were all laid out by the employers as part of a common plan.

Work has not only shaped people in Connecticut; people have also organized to reshape work. In 1867, Connecticut was the first state to legislate an eight-hour day, although an amendment to the law made it ineffective in practice. Labor organizations in the state date to the early 1800s; in 1885 the leading labor organization of the day, the Knights of Labor, claimed 60,000 members and elected 37 members to the Connecticut General Assembly. By the 1940s, most Connecticut industries were thoroughly unionized. As employment has shifted to non-industrial work since 1950, so the fastest growing unions have been in clerical work, education, and other service occupations.

I

The Diary of Joshua Hempsted

Joshua Hempsted (1678-1758), of New London, was a farmer, surveyor, house and ship carpenter, attorney, stone-cutter, sailor and trader. Excerpts from his diary, kept from 1711 to 1758, show the control this colonial craftsman had over his work and the way it was integrated into the rest of his life. He freely interrupted his work to undertake such civic responsibilities as attending town meetings and serving on juries. While some products were bought and sold, Hempsted also directly exchanged his labor; for example, he traded carpentry work for shoemaking.

1711

September 8th, Saturday.

Fair & Lowering. I worked at ye Ship about ye Stern, except 3 hours or less a making 15 foot Rails for ye Stern.

Monday, 10th.

I worked at ye Ship 3 hours or more...& came home. It Rained. I went to work about casements & for Joseph Truman at his house for him to make a pair of] Shoes for Joney.

Tuesday, 11th.

Fair. In ye forenoon I worked at home about Sol Coits Casements in ye afternoon at ye freemens meeting & making up accounts with Thomas Joans Collector & we paid Mr. Adams 25 pounds, 15 shillings, forenoon I worked at home about hay & Casements & in ye afternoon I was at Court to serve on ye Jury.

Tuesday, 18th.

Fair lowering. I did but little work only fitting in some casements for Sol. Coit & spent some time with Atwood & Parke at Shopleys about my land at Stonington. Parke offered me 210 pounds for my 200 acres.

Wednesday, 19th.

Fair I mowed & Cut Stalks.

I was at home all day I met with Some hurt with a Cow which having Newly Calved [and] being Angry Ran at me, Struck me in the face, Locked my teeth & Cut my lip & hurt my Arm & Leg. She Ripped off Molly's Gown & tore her Stays but did her no hurt.

Thursday, 20th.

Fair. I mowed & put in Joseph Truman's Window in ye forenoon & in ye afternoon I went to Get Timber for ye Belfrey Sills. I sent my white cow pasture at Jasper Rogers for 6 pence per week.

Saturday, 22nd.

Lowering. I Rake hay in Smiths Lot & gathered apples & carried [them] to Joseph Truman's mill.

Monday, 24th.

Fair. In ye forenoon I went to Holmes Lot to gather apples. I had but about 4 bushels & toward night I made a barrel [of] Cider.

Tuesday, 25th.

Superior court was first held in New London at ye meeting house. I was summoned to attend as juryman at eight of ye clock in ye morning. I pressed two Barrels [of] Cider at Joseph Truman's.

Friday, 28th.

Lowering. I worked at home all day stacking hay & oats. Little wind.

Saturday, 29th.

Fair, windy. In ye forepart of ye day till 2 or 3 o'Clock I went to get ye Sills of ye Belfrey Carted & to fetch 2 Swine from G. Chapells but could not catch ye biggest & in ye Later part of ye day I made a hog Sty etc.

Monday, October 1st.

Fair. I was Shoeing my Dray 'til about 2 o'clock & then I went into ye woods & got hewed 4 Sleepers for ye bark Lean to. At night we husked about a Load & 1/2 corn.

Tuesday, 2nd.

Fair. I picked out Corn & made a Platform to Lay ye husks on & I gathered some corn.

Wednesday, 3rd.

Fair. I went to mill & gathered corn.

Thursday, 4th.

Fair. I gathered corn in ye Lot at home & finished.

Friday, 5th.

Fair. I gathered Corn in Smith's Lot & we husked ye corn that grew in my Lot at night. A very windy day & Late in ye night it Rained a Little.

Saturday, 6th.

In ye morning Squally Little Rain. I finished gathering corn in Smith's Lot.

1729

April 1st, Tuesday.

Fair. I Set out for Colchester before day. I Arrived & went to measuring land.

Wednesday, 2nd.

I finished Measuring my land & it holds out 181 Acres which I have Sold to Joseph Dewey for 173 pounds to be paid by ye first of May or Else void.

Saturday, 5th.

All fair. I was helping Mr. Dewey Survey his land & Making a Map. I came away from Kelloggs at night.

Saturday, 12th.

Fair. I was at home Sowing oats & helping Rectify Ms. Sarah Christopher's fence digging up stones & out to Clement Minors.

Monday, 14th.

Fair. I was at home digging Stones.

Tuesday, 15th.

Stormy Rain. I was at home all day. Made 2 Shovels.

Wednesday, 16th.

Fair. I was at home all day digging Stones & breaking dung in ye lot.

Thursday, 17th.

Fair. I was at home & in Town. I finished Sowing oats, 1 Acre.

Saturday, 19th.

A Rainy Day. I went to [the] Mill. I got 1 1/2 bushels wheat ground & 2 bushels yesterday.

May 1st, Thursday.

Fair. I mended the fence in ye fore round ye old Orchard & after[wards] came home.

Monday, 5th.

Fair. I went to Groton to a freeholders Court at the house of Mr. Gardiner's to Assist the freeholders in Reviewing the Bounds of 2 acres of land at Poquonock plain.

Tuesday, 6th

I went with John Richards (a freeholder) to Stonington.

Wednesday, 8th.

Fair. We lodged at Capt. Daniel Denison's last night & [were] all day with the Selectmen & Divers[e] others viewing the road through the Town by an order of the C. Court in order to See the Necessity of Altering or relaying Said Road. We Received 16 shillings Each & came home at night. I also Received 25 shillings of Mr. Gardiner for Time & writing, etc.

Thursday, 8th.

Fair. I was at home all day I met with Some hurt with a Cow which having Newly Calved [and] being Angry Ran at me, Struck me in the face, Locked my teeth & Cut my lip & hurt my Arm & Leg. She Ripped off Molly's Gown & tore her Stays but did her no hurt.

Friday 9th & Saturday 10th.

Fair but rain last night. I was at home both days not well. Something of the fever & Ague [flu] both days.

1758

Tuesday, October 3rd.

Fair. I was out to Ebe Roger's, the great pasture, & fetched home the oxen, etc.

Wednesday, 4th.

Fair. I was about home most of the Day. We are gathering all the apples. Thomas in the orchard & Adam in the Lot yesterday, Shaking down, & Today picking up. We had Collin lee's Cart. I mended it 3 new Rounds. Adam carried a Jag [small load] of apples to Chapel's.

Saturday, 7th.

Fair. I was at home all day Trimming Cask[s], etc.

Friday, 20th.

Fair. I was at home all day. I Emptied 5 Barrels of Cider & filled one Hogshead [large barrel]. Adam carted home 2 Load[s] of Pumpkin from Chapman's.

Friday, 27th.

Cloudy. I was out to the cornfield all Day. I finished fencing 3 Stockyards all there. Raw cold.

Saturday, 28th.

Fair. I was most of the Day Stacking Corn Top in Crossman's Lot. Adam carted them & I handled Every Sheaf & Stowed them away & afterward we Loaded the Cart with a Small Stack of Clover & brought home to ye Barn.

Sunday, 29th, Cloudy.

I kept house at home all day, much Indisposed. A pain in my Bowels [has] been handing about me 2 or 3 days. Mond 30 fair. I am Still poorly. Keep about home all Day. Adam & Tommy went to the Salt meadow & fetch[ed] away the Salt hay that was left the about 30 Cocks—Josh & Neddy come over & brought my 2 Bay young Horse[s].

Tuesday, 31st.

Fair. I Rode down to Crossman & unloaded the Bigger part of the Salt hay. Night came & we left all to the weather.

Wednesday, November 1st.

Tommy helped unload. I Keep house.

Thursday, 2nd.

Fair. I was about home. Daughter Starr Sat up all night & with me all day Nursing me & Sat up all night again.

Friday, 3rd.

Fair. I keep house Still. Exceeding Sore in my bowels where the pain was last week. There is my difficulty. Daughter Starr Stands by me up all night again.

Joshua Hempsted died on December 22, 1758.

Tom Beardsley

The Hempsted house in New London, above, was built in 1678, the year Joshua Hempsted was born. An earlier house existed on the site, Joshua being the third generation of his family to live here. His son built an extension onto the house in the early 1700s. It remained in the Hempsted family until the death of Anna Hempsted Branch (1875-1937), a well known feminist and poet who was actively involved in suffragette politics and the settlement house movement in New York City. She indicated that this historic house should be opened to the public after her death.

The Joshua Hempsted House has been administered by the Connecticut Antiquarian and Landmarks Society since the late 1930s. It was completely renovated in the early 1950s. The site also consists of a stone house, known locally as the Huegenot House, built by Joshua's grandson, Nathan in 1757. The houses are open to the public on Friday, Saturday and Sunday, 12 until 5, between mid-May and mid-October, and by special appointment.

II

The Journal of Simeon Lymon of Sharon, August 10 — December 28, 1775

The working lives of Connecticut's residents was interrupted by British Redcoats sent by King George to quell democratic rumblings in the colonies. The following excerpts chronicle the experiences of Simeon Lymon, a young farmhand recruited during the American Revolutionary War. The occupation of soldier was common in colonial Connecticut where a series of conflicts with the French and Indians throughout much of the period kept many citizens under arms. Lyman's account presents a more mundane view of the conflict than the standard history text, presented as it is from the perspective of an obscure foot soldier doing the work of war.

August 11th, 1775.

We stayed at Litchfield 'til about 4 o'clock, there we had a sermon preached to us by Mr. Bellowmy, which I think I never heard outdone by anybody in my life, for liberty. He preached from Matthew 12th. Then we marched to Phillips about 8 miles into Torrington, there we kept guard all night.

August 12th.

The next morning we came to the tavern about 6 miles; there we went to breakfast. Then we went to Farmington, about 12 miles; there we stayed all night at Landlord Porter's. Sunday morning, 13th. We marched to Hartford, about 12 miles to Cromwell, there we heard a sermon in the afternoon. Then we went into the boat about 4 o'clock and we went to Rocky Hill, about 6 miles; there we stayed that night.

August 14th.

The next morning we went to Middletown: there we had a breakfast, then we went to Hadlyme and stayed that night.

August 15th.

The next morning we set off and we sailed down to the lower end of Lyme, then we went to shore and set off afoot and marched down to New London at the upper end of the town.

August 17th.

In the forenoon we walked round the town, and in the afternoon we was called to arms and were up to the meeting house, and there were about 200 weight of tea brought and put in the

In the morning it rained, and we heard about 220 great guns fired at Stonnington, and about noon there was a post came that (the British) was a firing at the town.

middle of the road, and there were tar barrels and shavings and wood put on, and then fire was put to it and consumed. There was about 400 soldiers under arms marched round 4 square, and there was a vast number of people and spectators around, some on houses and some on the walk of the meeting house, with a French horn and drums and fifes. They marched around the fire, and there were two that were with the tea that was blackened that came with the tea that was a running round on their heads, and so they continued till it was consumed, and came home.

August 19th.

We washed our clothes in the forenoon, and in the afternoon we marched out and exercised a while and came in, then there were 12 of us that were called out to guard the town.

August 20th.

Sunday morning we got ready for to go to meeting, and the officers came and said that we must not go to meeting without breeches, and it was so hot that I could not bear to wear them, and I did not go meeting in the forenoon. I went to see a crazy man and there was a man that knew him, and he got mad, and I think I never saw such a sight in my life. He was chained and he would spring at us and hallo at us. There was one stout man that said that he never saw a man that he was afraid of before. In the afternoon I went to meeting.

August 21st.

In the morning we marched out about 3 quarters of a mile, then we fixed our guns, and in the afternoon we marched out about a mile and exercised, and just before night we discovered a ship, and they sailed around the lighthouse, and about 12 o'clock there came a post that they were agoing to land, and there was no small stir among the people, and we had not drawed our powder, and our orders was that all that had powder and ball should fix out, and the companies got together about 186, and our captain was head, and the ensign was with him, and Sergeant Porter and a corporal and 4 solders, that was all that could fix out and they marched about sunrise 22 men , and about 8 o'clock they came in. The ship went off about daylight. In the afternoon we went off a-sailing.

August 25th.

In the morning we marched out before breakfast and we heard three great guns off on the Sound, and at night we heard 3 more, and we heard that they was chasing a brig.

August 30th.

In the morning it rained, and we heard about 220 great guns fired at Stonington, and about noon there was a post came that they was a firing at the town and that we must be ready at a minute's warning, and they got ready to march, and about 2 o'clock we had orders that half of the companies must go, and they marched round in a single file and counted off 20 men and went off.

August 31st.

In the morning they fired some cannon and went out to sea and come in sign of us. There came a post to us that they had not hurt but 3 or our men and had gone off. They did not hurt the town much. The people were a moving all day as fast as possible out of New London.

September 1st, A.D. 1775.

In the forenoon we went down to the lighthouse with our spyglass to see the ship, and we looked off and we see the Rose man of war and 3 sloops that they took from Stonington with 2 tenders. They all lay at anchor, and about 3 o'clock Mr. Shaw had a sloop that set sail, and when they came in reach of the ship they fired a gun and hailed them, and one of the tenders came and fetched them in to the ship and they all hoisted sail and came in plain sight of the town, and we was all ordered to get all our things together as quick as we could by the mayor, and we got them all in a heap, and the ship went round the island and it was so late that it could not go off, and we carried our packs in our old store.

Friday the 8th.

In the forenoon I dug a well and got 8 pence, and in the afternoon there came two companies to town and we had orders to come out of town to go to Lyme, and some of us came by water and the rest by land, and those that came by water was as sea sick as ever I see men in my life. I was sick with the rest. We

Tom Beardsley

The memorial above recounts a later clash with the British at the strategic town of Stonington during the war of 1812, When a landing force from HMS *Ramilles* was repulsed in 1814. In 1775, Simeon Lyman heard a skirmish between the Stonington militia, commanded by Oliver Smith and William Stanton, and the British frigate *Rose*, commanded by Captain James Wallace. The *Rose* was requisitioning supplies from the colonists on Block Island, but a subsequent threat to Stonington was resisted by the local militia.

had a very good wind, and we went round Fisher's Island about 40 miles, and we arrived at New London at night to our old tent to our great joy with the rest of our soldiers.

Saturday the 9th.

In the forenoon I washed my clothes and in the afternoon we had orders to march to Lyme, and we put all our things in our packs and put them aboard of a sloop, and about 3 o'clock we marched off about 4 miles and stayed at the tavern.

Saturday, 16th.

I was upon guard, and it rained all night. Our house leaked and we got wet through. I stood 3 times, 2 hours at a time. In the afternoon we heard 10 great guns off to the west on the Sound.

Sunday, 17th.

I went to meeting, and when we came home we had orders to go to Boston immediately.

Monday, 18th.

We were getting ready to move. We put up all our things ready to start off.

Tuesday, 19th.

We carried our packs down to the water to put them aboard, and about half of the soldiers went by water and the rest by land and we sat off and got almost there, and it began to rain and we got some wet. We got to New London about 4 o'clock, and we stayed to our old habitation that night.

Wednesday, 20th.

We looked round the town, and about 8 o'clock at night our sloop came ashore with the rest of our soldiers.

Thursday, 21st.

In the morning we moved our packs in another sloop to go to Norwich, and about 10 o'clock we marched off by land and we got to Norwich Landing about 4 o'clock. There we stayed that night.

Friday, 22nd.

We got our breakfast and set off and marched 8 miles, and it rained, and we staid at Captain Bornam's that night. I see a clock that would play tunes with 10 hammers, and a loom that wove stockings.

Saturday, 23rd.

In the morning we got some victuals, and marched 7 miles into Plainfield and ate again, then to Voluntown, about 12 miles...and got supper.

Sunday, 24th.

Morning, we got our breakfast and marched 8 miles to Coventry, Rhode Island, then we marched 6 miles and stayed that night. There were 2 companies that stayed there that night and got supper, and Monday 25th the next morning we marched to Johnston, then to Providence, and we marched through, in order, 2 miles. The streets were paved and houses as thick as they could well stand, and many things to see. Then to Pawtucket and then to Attleboro; there we stayed that night.

A few days later the company arrived in Boston. After a few skirmishes with British regulars on Bunker Hill, they trekked to western Massachusetts, and on Monday, December 18th, Simeon Lyman arrived home, and was reunited with family and friends. He traded in the occupation of soldier for that of farmhand once more.

III

George Bartholomew

Peddlers were the distribution system for eighteenth and nineteenth century commerce. In the days before transportation networks—canals, railroads, and later truck and airline routes—had been established, the Yankee peddler supplied manufactured goods to consumers who lived far from factories or stores. Goods produced in Connecticut were peddled not only in the state but in many other parts of the country. The following letters reveal some of the problems faced by these early traveling salespeople. They are from the correspondence sent to Mr. George Rennselaer Upson, of Bristol, CT, a farmer who spent part of his time as an agent for Mr. George Bartholomew, a peddler (also from Bristol), in the late 1820s. In the early 1830s he became a partner in a clock factory, and hired peddlers to sell the clocks in the Mississippi and Tennessee valleys.

Letters of George Bartholomew to Mr. R. Upson:

Athens, Alabama, December 27, 1825

I shall want you to forward some goods in the spring early or I shall have a slim assortment and you must get credit for a year. I shall get no money through the summer or not more than enough to pay freight and other expenses. I shall have about seventy dollars to pay on what you have shipped They came about six hundred miles by land the water was so low.

Mt. Zion, Mississippi, January 29, 1826

I shall be obliged to put you to some inconvenience in the payment of those debts in New York for the waters continue so low that the Planters cannot ship their cotton and the country is at present drained of money. I have enough due me to pay up for the whole, and if the waters have rose as soon as usual I should have been able to have met your contracts. I shall not credit much more until I make my collections. I have employed a man to go into the Choctaw Nation to trade for beaver and otter skins which the Indians have in abundance, and I am going another way to trade for the same. I think I can make something on them besides my profit on the goods by carrying them then to Huntsville and so turn my goods into money this spring. I can see no better chance for trade at present.

Respecting the 30 Clocks Shipped last fall, they arrived in Ohio late this Spring. The wires were very rusty and many of them were Swelled So that they will not run until I whittle & Smooth the wheels.

Athens, Alabama, May 28, 1826

The Goods I wrote you to send me in March I have not heard from yet but if they are not on the way yet I shall have nothing to Do before they get here, for my Goods are or will be scarce before long. You must be sure to send the fall Goods in season for should it continue dry the country is so situated that the merchants cannot Get goods until next spring freshets.

Athens, Alabama, September 4, 1826

You requested that I inform you what the prospects are for the coming season. I hardly know what to tell you but this much I think: it is the hardest times Alabama ever experienced and there is not a good prospect of it being much better. In some places the crops are very good but generally quite inferior, crops being short and a prospect of getting but a low price makes business very dull.

Athens, Alabama, October 22, 1826

Finally I have received the goods you purchased in June. I had not heard from them until last Thursday since they left Wheeling, which was the 8th August. Last Thursday I received a letter from Florence stating they were there; I started immediately after them. They were shipped from Lewisville on the 2 Sept. on board a keel boat. The captain and hands were taken sick and they were forty days getting to Florence and a week from the time they landed before they got here, which makes a trip of Four months lacking one day from New York.

Business is remarkably dull. I expect to have hard time of collecting next spring but there is no chance for doing business otherwise than on credit—and very slow at that—Cotton is a selling at $1 and $1.25 in the seed for cash. Mr. P. Barns thinks that the present crop will not pay up last Christmas's debts. This will make cracking times among the farmers for the merchants like the farmers are one year behind their contracts and are determined and obliged to make close collections this spring. Alabama is and will be for eighteen months to come the poorest state in the union for peddlers to do business in.

Columbus, Mississippi, January 16, 1827

I have once been taken up and fined one hundred dollars for peddling without a license but soon found the proceedings to be illegal and recovered the money again without any cost, which mortified the informer very much for he had made use of his part of the money and had to borrow it to pay it back.

I shall be obliged to disappoint you in your wishes with respect to making a final settlement of business this spring, the time of my credit having expired. I have been a trying for some weeks past to sell goods for cash but I find it out of the question. I certainly believe it would take me until Christmas to sell the balance of my goods for money down. At this time the people that want goods are those that have no money and are owing every dollar they will get for their cotton. I can sell the balance of my goods on a credit line until next Christmas at a handsome profit to good customers and be able I think to leave here by middle of April. If nothing happens this course I shall be obliged to pursue or keep the goods. You know well the difficulty of selling property for cash at the time you was in this country. Compare the times then with the present times and admit every merchant in this country to be a selling on a years credit and you can faintly imagine the difficulty of getting hold of a dollar which you have not a bond for.

I have been a trying for some weeks past to sell goods for cash but I find it out of the question...You know well the difficulty of selling property for cash at the time you was in this country.

Letter of George Bartholomew to R. Upson, Merrimans & Co.

Canton, Ohio, August 10, 1827

Respecting the 30 Clocks Shipped last fall, they arrived in Ohio late this Spring. The wires were very rusty and many of them were Swelled So that they will not run until I whittle & Smooth the wheels [Connecticut clocks at the time were primarily of wooden construction] of what I have sold which is 10, only 1 of that number was in order for running without being tinkered more or less. If I had been aware of the situation they were in I should not have been anxious to have had anything to do with them but I have paid the freight on them which was very high & I am a trying to Sell them.

IV

Lucius Bigelow

With the creation of extensive transportation systems, from canals to railroads, and more sophisticated distribution networks, peddling went into a decline and by the late 1800s there were very few peddlers left, having been replaced by the traveling sales representatives for specific products. In 1965, Martha Zablocki, Simsbury schoolteacher, interviewed Walter Gillette, the nephew of Lucius Bigelow (1842-1932) of Weatogue, described as "one of the last of the Yankee tin peddlers," who plied his trade after his return from the Civil War, until 1929. Mr. Gillette recounts boyhood experiences traveling with his uncle on his rounds, and Mrs. Gillette adds additional insights from her own memories. [Bigelow's original tin cart is housed at the Simsbury Historical Society, along with the tape recorded interview of Mr. and Mrs. Gillette.]

Martha Zablocki: I am at the home of Mr. and Mrs. Walter Gillette of Hopmeadow St., Simsbury. Mr. Gillette is the nephew of Mr. Lucius W. Bigelow, Civil War veteran and Yankee tin peddler, the last one in this vicinity to ply his trade. Mr. Bigelow was your uncle, Mr. Gillette, isn't that so?

Walter Gillette: Yes, Ma'am.

MZ: I knew that he lived in the house near the Pettibone Tavern, but I believe he lived elsewhere prior to his purchase of that home.

WG: When I first knew my uncle, he lived in the Gillette homestead on South Main Street. Moving from there he went to Dr. Barbour House out on North Main Street, opposite the high school. From the high school home, Dr. Barbour's, he went to Weatogue, where he resided until his death.

MZ: Mr. Gillette, you were fortunate in that you actually went around with Mr. Bigelow on his route. Would you tell us about that?

WG: Well, he had a route that consisted of suburban towns—Avon, Farmington, Unionville, Burlington, Collinsville, New Hartford, Pine Meadow, Canton, Canton Center, North Canton, Granby, North Granby, West Granby, Bloomfield, North Bloomfield, and Simsbury.

We were very amused to see him lift the covers off of the tin cart, and we saw all the displays of washboards and tubs, and dippers, and tea strainers, and everything that one could imagine in a household. I imagine that the housewife would just like to have had everything on it.

MZ: That's very interesting. Did he do all that in one day?

WG: No, ma'am. He used to go sometimes and stay a week at a time, at different places.

MZ: And where did he stay overnight?

WG: He stayed at some of his customers' houses.

MZ: Do you suppose he paid for his room and board, or did he exchange his room and board for something on his cart?

WG: I imagine he exchanged.

MZ: Mrs. [Maisy] Viets of East Granby told me that Mr. Bigelow spent the night at her mother's house. That's just one place that he stayed. Could you tell us the names of any other folks where he stayed?

WG: He stayed at the house of a man by the name of Edsel Foote in Canton Center. He also used to stay at a man named High Adams, that was over in East Granby.

MZ: We know that the cart carried tinware, and I have right in front of me, I am handling right now an agate sauce pan, I guess you'd call it, wouldn't you, Mrs. Gillette?

Mrs. Gillette: I think it is.

MZ: That came off the tin cart. And it's well-preserved, but I can imagine that many a wonderful dish has been prepared in this agate pan. There must have been many other Yankee notions on the cart. Can you tell us what else was on the cart, Mr. Gillette?

WG: Well, he carried brooms, bedroom lamps, kerosene lanterns, milk pails, saucepans, measuring cups for measuring liquids.

MZ: Did he carry any foods at all?

WG: Not that I know of.

MZ: How did the housewives know that he was coming? Did he have a horn or a bell of some kind?

WG: No, he'd generally stop at the house and go in.

MZ: I would think that the tinware would make enough noise for anybody to hear it as he came along. Was that so?

WG: Well, he had it packed in compartments, certain sizes for a certain size dish.

MZ: Where did Mr. Bigelow purchase the items that he sold?

WG: I think most of them was purchased over in Winsted way.

MZ: Mrs. Gillette, did you remember Mr. Bigelow as he came through Collinsville?

MG: I do. I remember when I was going to school, Mr. Bigelow used to stop his cart and unhitch the horse to feed him. He would have his lunch. And all of the school chums would go up and sit beside him, and he would take the brooms off, and let us hold them—which we only wished we could have one. And it was fascinating because then he had this white horse that he thought a lot of.

MZ: There was just one horse with a cart?

MG: That's all. And we were very amused to see him lift the covers off of the tin cart, and we saw all the displays of washboards and tubs, and dippers, and tea strainers, and everything that one could imagine in a household. I imagine that the housewife would just like to have had everything on it.

MZ: Did you have any idea how much some of the items costs?

MG: I don't have any idea. Because I remember I was real young then. My mother always bought something, but I imagine it was pie tins or dippers or some useful thing she needed.

MZ: Did he just carry his own lunch with him?

MG: Yes, he carried his lunch with him. And he always used to ask us if we had any old rubbers, to be sure and save them, because that's what he was after. Of course, in those days, we wore a lot of rubbers. We didn't wear galoshes like today.

MZ: Was Mr. Bigelow's cart made in Simsbury, Mr. Gillete?

WG: No, ma'am, it was made in Westfield, Massachusetts.

MZ: I believe Westfield did make carts and whips at that time.

WG: That is correct.

MZ: Mr. Gillette, did you go along just for the ride, or did you have some chores when you rode the cart?

WG: Well, I went for the ride, and I also went because he let me drive the horse.

MZ: What sort of man was Mr. Bigelow?

MG: Well, Mr. Bigelow was a very quiet man, gentle and very lovable, and a man that always liked a lot of people around. And he was a very interesting man because he, so many times, talked about when he was in the Civil War.

MZ: Yes, I believe you told us, Mr. Gillette, that Mr. Bigelow enlisted at an early age — how old was he?

WG: Sixteen years of age.

MZ: And that he lied about his age to get in at that time.

WG: That's what he told me.

MZ: And he lived to be of a ripe old age. Do you recall how old he was when he died?

WG: Ninety.

MZ: I imagine that Mrs. Bigelow was glad to see her husband after he had completed his route.

WG: Yes, she was always glad to see him come home.

MZ: What did he do when he got home?

WG: He'd sort the rags and the rubbers, the copper, zinc and lead that he'd purchased on his route. Then he'd restock his cart and he'd start off again.

MZ: I imagine that Mr. Bigelow had a tidy sum of coins and bills after a day's run. Did he keep the money in a cigar box?

WG: No, he had a tin cashbox. If it was silver, he put it under the seat. And his bills—he had a slip in the horse collar, and he'd put the bills in there, so in case he was held up, why, he had but little money on his person.

MZ: Well, he was very clever. I suppose people had to be careful in those days, too. You suppose that horse collar is around anywhere?

WG: No, I don't imagine so.

MZ: Mrs. Gillette, tell us about Mr. Bigelow's liking to fuss around in the kitchen.

MG: Oh, Mr. Bigelow used to like to pare vegetables, and get 'em ready for dinner. And then he always delighted in doing dishes. And his one great ambition was to always polish the old black kitchen stove, and that was a thing that he always liked to do. But, if there was any chores around the house, he delighted in doing what was in the kitchen work.

MZ: Mr. Gillette, you mentioned the fact that Mr. Bigelow collected and sold antiques along with the tinware.

WG: That's right. He would purchase antiques when he was on his route, bring them home, refinish them and then resell 'em.

MG: And then Mr. Bigelow also had cases, like showcases, in his dining room, and he would pick up antiques, and then price them. And people that he used to go on the routes that came there from near and far, and used to purchase them.

MZ: That's interesting. I wonder if any of those are now in the Simsbury Historical Society. Would you know that, Mrs. Gillette?

MG: I don't know. I know I have one that he gave me that I have. I don't have it in sight, for no reason, it's just that I put it away. It's a little vase. It's small, white glazed.

MZ: It must be a lovely keepsake.

MG: That is why I'm keeping it.

MZ: That's very nice. Well, we're very grateful to you, Mr. and Mrs. Gillette, for this afternoon, and giving us this intimate glimpse of Mr. Gillette's uncle, Mr. Lucius W. Bigelow, who was the last of the tin peddlers. Thank you very much.

Simsbury Historical Society

Lucius Bigelow is pictured above on his peddler's cart, c 1920. The cart was donated to the Simsbury Historical Society in September 1934 by his widow, where it can still be viewed. The cart was prominently featured at the Connecticut Tercentenary Exposition in 1935, to highlight the "Yankee Peddlar." The cart also appeared on the cover of the October 1935 issue of the magazine *Connecticut Industry*, wherein readers were reminded that Yankee peddlars were "an essential factor in the growth of industry in the state between 1740 and 1860."

V

Arthur Botsford

Among Connecticut's many traditional occupations, clockmaking has undergone drastic changes since it began as a cottage industry in towns like Thomaston and Bristol in the 1700s. From wooden to metal parts—and finally electronic chips, the nature of the production process—and the relationship of workers to that process—bears little resemblance to the original craft of making timepieces.

Arthur Botsford, Litchfield Street, Thomaston, CT, who retired from active work in the spring of 1938, after a clockmaking career that started when he was fifteen and continued for sixty-five years, acts as informal historian, when interviewed for the W.P.A. Federal Writers Project [c.1939]. Passages in italics are the interviewer's comments from the original transcript.

My father came here in 1847 from South Britain (Conn.). I can remember hearin' him tell about the first railway through these parts and how he and some others walked all the way from South Britain to down around Seymour, or some such place, to see the first train. My dad worked for Sanford four years after he came here and then he got in the clock shop and worked there till he died.

They started making tower clocks sometime in the seventies. They built the Centennial Clock in '76, the one that went to Independence Hall, Philadelphia. The two big Colgate clocks are probably their most famous products.

There were two places in town and one in Plymouth where they used to make clock parts—not the complete articles, understand—but just parts. I guess they sold to Seth Thomas, yes, I presume like that was the principal market. One of the factories was owned by Sam Sanford over there on the corner of the street that's named after him—"Sanford Avenue."

They made pendulum rods, wire bells, and verges there. I worked over in the Movement Shop. Seth Thomas—you talk about fables and I'll tell you what always used to pass for gospel truth, but I think it's a fable—Seth Thomas, they said, came here afoot from Wolcott, where he was born, carrying all his belongings in a bandana knotted at the end of a stick. And they said—though I don't say this couldn't be done, mind you—they said he whittled the first clock he ever made with a jack-knife—whittled the whole darn thing entire. *At this point Mr. Bostford produced a tiny peach stone, whittled into the semblance of a monkey. It was a creditable piece of work and he was obviously proud of it.* If a man could do that, why couldn't he whittle a clock part.

Thomaston Library

Seth Thomas, 1813-1850, Yankee clock maker, and founder of the Seth Thomas Clock Company

Anyway, I don't know what Seth's circumstances were when he come here, but before he died he owned pretty darn near the whole town. I can remember my dad telling about the big general store Seth ran up near the center of town. You paid for what you got once a year. At the end of that time, some of them owed him money—the ones that worked for him, I mean, they'd spent more than they'd earned. Sure, he took it out of their wages. Oh, he sold to others, too, the man didn't have to work for him to trade there. The post office was kept in that store, too.

It burned down, the whole building. Seth died in 1859. And when he died he owned plenty, not only buildings, but land and stock. The side hills was dotted with his sheep and cattle; he owned all the land around Marine and Litchfield Streets and Grand Street and through the center of the town.

Of course, there was other big landowners, too, had parcels here and there. There was the Alcotts, and R.T. Andrews, and the Blakelees, and across the river was the Potter place—they had a factory over in back there, the Potters did, where they manufactured guns—didn't know they was guns made in the early days in Connecticut, did you—and then where McGrath's is was the Marsh place and the Woodwards and the Judsons on High Street. But all they owned wasn't a patch on Seth's property.

Seth had Aaron and Seth and Edward and three girls, nears I can remember. Bill Woodruff's mother was one of the girls; she was a Thomas. And Ed Thomas had Walter and three girls, and all these kind of married with the other prominent families in town. Miles Morse, him that ran the clock shop I told you about the other day, he married one of them. They called him "Squire Morse." After he give up the clock business, he started up the knife shop, down to Reynolds' Bridge, and he lived in that big house they call the Mansion, right across the river. You can see it from the main road. Afterwards he built the big place in the center of town that was torn down this summer.

Seth Thomas as you know, came here in 1813. He built his shops and established his business then, but he acquired most of his property in the early thirties. Not many people remember now that the old man branched out into the cotton business at one time. The bell from the old Cotton Mill, by the way, made in Hartford in 1833, is still in the cellar of the old building that used to house the Thomaston National Bank on Elm Street.

Well, sir, they had to stop making cotton goods when the war broke out, and then they moved the clock metal works up to the old Cotton Mill and still continued to make the cases in what is known to this day as the Case Shop on South Main Street. Old Seth, by the way, used to buy his brass, but he couldn't get it when he wanted it. So he built the rolling mill, and that is now the Plume and Atwood Manufacturing Co. Not many people still remember that, either, and I doubt if you'll find many records of that transaction. It burned down in 1856, and was rebuilt the same year, and there is one shaft in operation today under the floor of that mill that was used in the original building. There's something for you to write about.

After the death of old Seth Thomas in 1859, the mill, as I said, passed into the hands of the Plume and Atwood Company. It used to be a treat for the people of this town—I can remember doing it as a boy—to go over to the mill and see the big engine. It was a regular waling-beam steamboat engine—imagine that—and they had stairs leading up to a little gallery where you could stand and watch it in operation.

Then sometime in the middle 1860s, they talked about making marine clocks. Some of the stockholders objected to the idea, thought they'd lose money on it—so they formed a new company—called it Seth Thomas Sons & Co., and they took the old sawmill in the west part of the town and built on to the west wing. But the dispute got settled or arbitrated or whatever you call it and shortly afterward they merged into one company again.

Marine clock? That was kind of a catch name, probably one of the earliest attempts at high pressure advertising. It was made with a balance wheel instead of pendulum. They had a slogan for it printed on advertising cards about the size of a postcard. It read: "It stands up, Lays down, and runs all the time." They called it "marine" simply because it would run on the ocean, same's it would on land.

That's how the old Marine shop got its name, and the Thomaston Marine Band, organized God knows how many years ago—more than 50 anyway, and made up of men who worked in the Marine shop. They began making watches there in the eighties, but they discontinued the watches in 1914. Then they moved the metal working department from the Movement shop to the Marine shop until 1938, when they moved the whole darn business down on South Main Street, under one roof.

They started making tower clocks sometime in the seventies. They built the Centennial Clock in '76, the one that went to Independence Hall, Philadelphia. The two big Colgate clocks are probably their most famous products. But first of all they made these. *Mr. Botsford produced an ancient wooden movement, of which he was obviously proud.* I could take this clock today, and put a pendulum and a dial on it and start it and I bet it'd keep perfect time. It ain't any good as an antique though because it's a 30-hour and collectors don't want nothin' but eight days.

Did I ever hear the old clockmakers use their own special names for anything? Can't say's I did. They used to call cannon pinions "center sockerts" and spring boxes "Barrels"—that's the sort of thing—but it didn't have any meaning.

Yes, I remember Aaron Thomas and one thing that sticks in my memory is an example of the famous temper Aaron had. He used to ride back and forth between the shops in horseback—had a horse that had seen Army service and carried a big brand on its flank. I was coming along the street one day and I see Aaron stop to talk to one of his farm workmen. The horse wouldn't stand still and Aaron—he had a strap hung with clockweights he was carrying from one shop to the other—and he just swung it down and thrashed that horse till it behaved. He had a high temper—and in some respects he was a peculiar man.

There's another thing I want to tell you about. Years ago there was a lot of deaf and dumb people working in the shops. Must have been as many as twenty or twenty-five of them. No, I don't know as they were any better clockmakers than ordinary folks. Reason they worked there I guess is that Frank Crossman, he used to be superintendent of one of the plants, had a deaf and dumb brother and he kind of felt sorry for them I guess, and gave them jobs.

I've got a steel engraving here of Seth Thomas. *Mr. Botsford brought out an album, turned a few pages, and pointed to the engraving. Mr. Thomas, encased to the chin in what used to be called a stock, I believe, and with long white sideburns and white hair combed in bangs over his forehead looked like a character from Dickens.* I got it out of one of the company's old catalogs, there ain't many pictures of old Seth around.

No there's no Swiss clockmakers in town, and none that ever came here, s'far as I know, but I tell you what happened after the Civil War. A lot of Germans came here and distributed themselves around. Some went to clock factories in Winsted and New Haven and some came here. They worked in this country quite a few years till they got the idea of clock manufacture, and then they started a big clock factory over in Germany. The Seth Thomas agent in London bought one of their clocks and sent it over here, and they found out it was patterned exactly after the Seth Thomas.

German clockmakers are good, individually, but they didn't know anything about mass production. Oh, yes, I'll grant you German clockmakers know their business. They have to be able to assemble a clock before they can call themselves clockmakers. But they had to copy American manufacturing. I saw the movement they sent over here, and that was in 1888. They say they had a monstrous big shop over there, biggest in the world.

And I'll tell you something else young fellow, back in the eighties someone in Meriden invented a metal pinion to be cast with gears and wheels completed. They peddled it around to the clock companies in this section without success—nobody could see it.

After a while a company started making them out in LaSalle, Illinois, and that company is now Westclox, which is the parent organization of General Times Instruments, which owns Seth Thomas. Figure that out. If Seth Thomas had bought that pinion maybe they'd still be making clocks on their own hook.

Tom Beardsley

The Seth Thomas Clock Company factory is still standing in downtown Thomaston—which is attractively situated in the Naugatuck River Valley in northwest Connecticut. This building now houses the Seth Thomas Industrial Park, the home of a number of small, modern companies. This kind of reuse is common across Connecticut, where large 19th and early 20th century mills and factories are being modified for small-scale operations.

VI

John Davis

Not only has work in general formed the backbone of family and community, but many families and communities have come to be defined by the particular kinds of work that they do. John Davis, a knife maker living in Thomaston, was not only part of a family of knifemakers from England, but also shared this occupation with a number of English immigrants living in the area. He was interviewed on March 14, 1939, for the W.P.A. Federal Writers' Project, by Francis Donovan who provided his own highly romanticized, but informative, introduction to his "subject":

"One of the few remaining craftsmen in these parts of a trade rapidly vanishing from the New England scene is John Davis, 76, of Pleasant Street, who learned knifemaking from his father. The elder Davis was a native of Sheffield, England, where knifemaking was invested with something of the dignity which attached to the medieval guilds, and was passed on with Masonic secrecy from generation to generation. Mr. Davis' father was a cutler, master tradesman of the craft, a calling comparable to that of the master clockmaker who is capable of performing any operation up to and including the final assembly of the movement. The Davis', father and son, worked both in Northfield and in the American Knife Company at Reynolds' Bridge, Thomaston, as well as others in this immediate section. But the younger Davis, having learned the trade, turned to clockmaking and worked in the knife factories only when the clock industry was 'slow.' "

Very peculiar men them Johnnies were. In the old country from what my father told me, they were so jealous of the trade, that you had to be a close relative of a knifemaker before he'd show you any-thing.

You hear mostly about the Northfield Knife company, but the old American Knife Company at Reynolds Bridge was the biggest around here. Old Mr. Pierpont and Squire Morse owned it when my father first worked there. And most of the knifemakers were from the old country. They had their own methods and they didn't give a damn about improvements, didn't want any. They made all their own drills. You'd seldom see a twist drill. They were all flat, filed onto stock and hardened and drawn. Old Pierpont and Morse, they thought that was all right too, because twist drills cost money.

They made pocket cutlery, and other knives, but they bought their shears and razors from another company. Had their trademark put on 'em. They had more hands down there when

Peck Manufacturing Company

Tom Beardsley

Above: Workers at the American Knife Company at Reynolds Bridge, Thomaston, pose for the camera in 1888. Many of them are from Sheffield, England, for many years, the world center for the manufacture of high quality stainless steel cutlery. Below: The site today, still the home of light industy in the form of Peck Manufacturing.

they were goin' good than they ever had at Northfield. They imported forty men from Sheffield, cutlers, grinders, forgers. They had five forgers when I worked there—and that was in the eighties—they had five hand forgers and one drop forger for drop work. Used all imported steel—right from Sheffield.

You see those Johnnies were very peculiar men in that way. Everything had to be as near as possible like what it was when they learned the trade in the old country. If anything went wrong they'd blame it on conditions in this country. They had a couple of men hardening blades, old Mr. Finkle and Lambert Savage. Had quite a bit of trouble with the blades one time they weren't turning out just right, and the foreman went to old Finkle and asked him what the trouble was. "It's this goddam American water," says old Finkle. "Can't do anything with water like this. We never worked with this kind of water."

Very peculiar men them Johnnies were. [Johnny is a diminutive for 'John Bull', the British cultural equivalent to 'Uncle Sam'] In the old country from what my father told me, they were so jealous of the trade, that you had to be a close relative of a knifemaker before he'd show you anything. And it was damn near as bad here. They used to do it all in the homes, over there. A knifemaker would go to a factory, and get a job, buy his material and go home and turn it out. Then somebody in the business began to make cheaper knives in what they called "gangs."

But the old timers that came over here could make knives from the bottom up. If a boss wanted a model he could go to any one of the men and get it done. They made all their own tools, and they stuck to the old ways of doing things and that's one of the reasons, they say, the business petered out. They wouldn't stand for any change. I've seen one of those old fellas work for hours with a breast drill and a wise, boring a hole, when he could have used the drill lathe. But no, by God, he learned to do it that way, and that's the way he was going to do it, even if it took him ten times as long.

Yes, they had knife factories all over this section of the state. And I think about the only place they still make pocket cutlery to any extend today is Landers Frary and Clark in New Britain. Look at all the others there used to be—one in Lakeville—that might be still going , I don't know—and one in Winsted, one in Southington, one in Northfield, one in Torrington, one down here at the Bridgeport, one in Hotchikissville, one in Middlebury, one in Cotton Hollow, one in Union City. Most of them were small places of course.

A lot of them used to import their labor from Sheffield before the United States passed a law preventing it. Some of them would get over here and renege on their contract. Figured they could get out of paying their passage money. I know one lad that tried it. But the first place he got a job—in one of the other shops—they docked his wages for the passage money. He found out they had an agreement, all the knife manufacturers. He'd have had to pay that money wherever he went.

Business went on the bum down here during Cleveland's first administration (1885-1889). Knives came in from Germany and Italy and sold cheap. It never seemed to get back to where it was after that. They had that free trade agreement or whatever they called it. The knife companies started slipping. But they wouldn't change. They wouldn't try to meet the competition with cheaper knives. They wouldn't do any different than the way they'd been taught. Nowadays they import the material all ready to assemble, I understand. They can make cheap knives, you can by 'em in the dime store, but they're no damn good.

Well the Johnnies learned their trade in a hard way and they stuck to it till it disappeared. They learned in what they called "little mester shops" in the old country. This was likely to be just a room in some knifemaker's house—just like the old clockmakers in Germany learned their trade. They did everything by hand. Got as much as six or seven dollars a dozen for some makes of knives and that was big money.

I've heard my father say that at Christmas time, when they had a big order to get out and wanted a little extra money for Christmas, they'd bring their wives in and put them to work. Made an awful lot of knives done here in the old plant for some mail order concern, I think it was the Henry Sears company. I suppose that's Sears Roebuck now.

Made better money than the clockmakers did. When they were getting a dollar and a quarter and a dollar and a half a day up here in the clock shop it was a dam poor man that couldn't make two dollars or better at the knife factory. All piece work. The forger got so much a gross and the hardener so much for hardening and tempering, and the grinder so much. The cutler had to assemble and finish the knife and finish the handle. Even the repairs were piece work. You got a good job on repairs, maybe just riveting blades or something like that, you could do probably a hundred a day at four cents a piece.

Old Mr. Perpont, I don't know if he knew anything about the business before he bought into it or not, but he knew plenty about it before he got through. I've seen him inspecting blades all day long just like one of the hands. Squire Morse's people used to make clocks.

The shop burned down once, but they built it up again and bought out the Connecticut cutlery company in Union City, moved all the machinery up here. That belonged to Tuttle and Whitmore. Then when the American Company shut the doors, Mr. Warner, who used to be secretary and bookkeeper, started a business in the old brick shop on the main road down here that used to be part of Terry's woolen mill. They used to hold dances in the top floor of that building, I remember. Of course that's burned down now, too.

Glad somebody's writin' all this down. It's a good thing to put on records. And if I can help you out again just let me know. Any time, any time at all. I got plenty of time these days.

VII

Albert Roth

Farming has continued to be a significant, if diminishing factor in the worklife of Connecticut. Albert John Roth, age 79, now living in Colchester, recalls a childhood spent on a small farm in Harwinton where, at the turn of this century, work tools and methods were still little affected by technological changes that have since changed agriculture dramatically.

The day began very early on our thirty-acre farm in rural Harwinton, Connecticut. Everyone in our family helped with feeding animals and milking cows. After these chores were completed, we would all come in to eat the hearty breakfast which my mother had prepared. After breakfast, it was out to the fields to hoe corn and gather vegetables. Even the small children did their part by picking berries and gathering eggs. How I hated those chores! Often, my friends would go by on their way to the swimming hole, while I was required to work. How I wished that I could go with them.

We installed a bathtub—a big improvement over bathing in a wash tub. Then came the best change of all, a flush toilet. This replaced our three-holer outhouse. When the word got around, all of our friends and neighbors came to see it, especially the kids, who wanted to use it so that they could see it work.

Every Saturday, my parents went to nearby Torrington in our surrey. There were six children in our family. One week, three of my sisters went with them, and the next week, my other two sisters and I were allowed to go. I was dazzled by the "big city" atmosphere—tall buildings, trolley cars, paved roads with electric street lights, delivery trucks, and specially the theater. Our first stop was always at the huge fountain in the center of town, where we watered our horse. Then, we left the horse in the horse shed behind our church, and walked to the theater. There we saw black and white, silent movies and also enjoyed five sparkling vaudeville acts, including comedy, dancing, juggling, and others. During the weeks that it was my turn to stay home, my sisters and I would amuse ourselves by making fudge. Sometimes the fudge didn't harden, and we would eat the gloppy candy with spoons.

When school was in session, we still did the before-breakfast chores before we walked to our close-by one-room school (school busses had not yet been invented). I was very excited when I became old enough to start school. My older sisters had told me how much fun it was to play with the other children at recess time. Our school was one of ten one-roomed schools in town. The families of school children were required to contribute wood to keep the wood stove going in the winter. The children took turns walking to our farm to get a pail of water for drinking. We all had to help sweep the floor and take out the ashes after school. The country schools at this time were large enough to accommodate about twenty or more students. One teacher taught all eight grades. What a hectic learning situation that was! Several years later, our school was enlarged to two rooms. This made for a much improved and a more pleasant learning experience. Now, my two older sisters and I were in the new addition, in the four upper grades. We no longer had to listen to recitations by all eight grades. However, I must say that there had been a definite plus side to the learning process in hearing the repeated lessons. We sometimes heard things we had missed in the lower grades, and also became acquainted with subjects we would eventually be learning in the upper grades. I developed a tremendous crush on my teacher, and often made excuses to stay after school for special help with my homework. To me, she was the most beautiful young lady in the world. The school years were much the same as now, September to June. I'm sure that this schedule was established for the obvious reason that farmers needed the children at home in the summer to help during the growing season—work that had to be accomplished before winter brought everything to a halt.

Tom Beardsley

The Clearview Avenue farmhouse in rural Harwinton which Albert Roth recalls from his childhood. Albert's father, John Roth, purchased the house and 30 acre farm in 1911.

Our farmhouse was the usual type with sections that were added from time to time to provide room for the growing family. It was heated by wood stoves and fireplaces. Our large living room was used only on Sundays, or when we had guests. The kitchen-dining room was more or less the family room. It had several tables which were used for doing homework, reading and for a variety of other tasks. The house was lighted by kerosene lamps, both table lamps and those mounted on the walls with magnifying mirrors behind them to make the light shine more brightly.

Another section of our house was a combination cooking, baking, and workroom, with a woodburning stove, and also a kerosene cookstove. There was also a cream separator, a hand-operated clothes washer, a butter churn, and other items needed for housekeeping chores. The most unusual thing in the room was a well with a pump. Next to it was a big water tank into which we put large containers for milk and other foods, to keep them cool in the icy water. Later, my parents bought an ice box. A delivery man came with a horse and wagon to bring us heavy chunks of ice for the ice box.

Obviously, chores and regular work had to be done every day of the year; but on Sundays and other important holidays, we did only the most necessary chores. The rest of the day was spent going to church, socializing, visiting neighbors and friends, and having picnics in the shade of the big apple tree. Late in the afternoon, we finished whatever work still needed to be done.

Tom Beardsley

The rural-urban comparison between Harwinton and Torrington is clear. Torrington can be seen in the Naugatuck Valley from a high vantage point in Harwinton, atop Twenty Four Bumper Road.

One of the most helpful things on the farm was our windmill. This wind-powered workhorse would pump water to a large eight-hundred gallon tank, located in a loft in our haybarn. In the winter, we stacked hay around it to keep the water from freezing. Only occasionally, when the weather was extreme, did it freeze a little on top. This water system was developed mainly to provide our cattle and other animals with a constant supply of water. This was a great time saver. Formerly, we had had to let the animals out of the barn to drink from the watering trough, and then had to put them back inside.

Eventually, my ingenious father extended this automatic, nonelectronic, water system into the house. Then wonderful things began to happen! First, we installed a bathtub—a big improvement over bathing in a wash tub. Then came the best change of all, a flush toilet. This replaced our three-holer outhouse. When the word got around, all of our friends and neighbors came to see it, especially the kids, who wanted to use it so that they could see it work. Our many visitors liked what they saw and began to follow our example, installing similar water systems, since electrical power was not yet available to the farmers at that time. Only a few people, in the higher income brackets, had electricity in our town. The first utility poles that were erected were for the telephone system only, not for power lines. The only power we had were some small one-cylinder gasoline engines, one of which ran our wood cutting saw. This was a delightful change from having to cut wood with a two-man six-foot crosscut hand saw.

We made space in our huge woodshed to house the 1917 Maxwell which my father bought second-hand for about three or four hundred dollars. This car was our pride and joy. It was driven only in the summer. It was put up on blocks during the winter. In those early days of cars, there were traveling mechanics who had been trained by the automobile manufacturers. When the car owner found that he was unable to repair his car by himself, he would call a mechanic to do the job. The mechanic was paid half the cost of repair by the company and half by the car owner. Sometimes the car manufacturer would supply the owner with free parts! Often, my father would allow me to help him repair the car. This experience promoted me to become a machinist. My chosen occupation eventually led to a career as a technical school instructor, a position I held for thirty years until my retirement.

From an 1988 essay contest, "Memories of Connecticut Life," sponsored by the Connecticut State Department on Aging.

Torrington Historical Society

Left: The Torrington which Albert Roth recalls is pictured in this view of the junction of East Main Street and Main Street, looking north, c. 1925. Roth recalls Torrington's big city atmosphere, "tall buildings, trolley cars, paved roads with electric street lights, delivery trucks, and specially the theater. Ou first stop was always at the huge fountain in the center of town, where we watered our horse."

Right: The same view in modern, post industrial Torrington. This historic city in northwest Connecticut identifies closely with the Civil War. It is the birthplace of abolitionist John Brown, whose raid on the federal arsenal at Harper's Ferry in 1859, helped to trigger the clash with the south. Torrington is also the home of Gail Borden, the founder of the Borden Company, who devised the formula for condensed milk—the milk that won the Civil War.

Tom Beardsley

VIII

Arthur Cockayne

There have been instances where the development of machine production still could involve the creative input of skilled craftspeople. This has been true in the lacemaking industry where large, complex machines can be programmed by skilled operators to produce great varieties of delicately woven lace. Arthur Cockayne, from a family of English lacemakers, describes his work with the machines and the Deep River Lace Factory, Deep River, Connecticut. Interviewed by Bruce M. Stave on June 18, 1981, for the "Connecticut Workers and Technology" oral history project, Mr. Cockayne's reminisences have been edited into narrative form.

I was born in Pawtucket, Rhode Island, on December 18, 1922. My father, he was born in Brooklyn, New York in 1896. His father, my grandfather, Roland, he was born in Long Eaton, England; he came to this country in about 1892. He was in lace, the same thing I'm doing. A lace weaver, a twist hand, has to set up and operate a Weaver's lace machine. All of the equipment here came from England, it was made in England, everything that's in here. It is basically the same machinery, with minor improvements here and there, and it's run on an electric motor instead of a waterfall.

All of the equipment here came from England, it was made in England, everything that's in here...my mother's father was a draftsman for the lace industry. He drew the lace patterns. He came from Long Eaton. It's outside Nottingham. That's where most of the trade came from.

One of the first lace factories in this country was in Brooklyn, New York, and my grandfather came over to work in it. My father was also in the trade. Well, not long after my dad was born, my grandfather and the family moved to Pawtucket, Rhode Island. The traders decided to import from England to Rhode Island, and he went there to work, and, of course, as my dad grew up he worked in Rhode Island. And then about 1925 my father and two of my uncles, my mother's brother and my mother's sister's brother, started a lace factory of their own in Rockville, Connecticut. It's gone now. But they started around there from 1925 till 1938 when the hurricane blew the roof off the place and that was it, it was all over. They were pretty strapped from the thing folding up. So then they went back to Rhode Island again and my dad worked in the trade then till he retired.

Then on my mother's side, my mother's father was a draftsman for the lace industry. He drew the lace patterns. He came from Long Eaton. It's outside Nottingham. That's where most of the trade came from. My father's father was also from Long Eaton, but my dad and mother were married in this country.

My mother came to this country in 1912. Her family was in the lace trade—more in the drafting and designing end of it. They didn't have too much to do with the operation of the machinery. In fact, my mother's older brother studied the drafting and designing in France where there was quite a bit of lace trade in there. Most of all the machinery was made in England, but there was a lot of drafting done in France, and a lot of the English machines went to France, too, they were operated in France. In fact, even today, I guess, there's quite a few in France.

I went to elementary school and most of high school in Rockville, Connecticut, and then because we moved to Rhode Island I finished high school in West Warwick, Rhode Island. And then I went in the Navy for four years, and I come out and I worked in the lace trade with my dad until 1948. I then came down here to Deep River. It was a three-year apprenticeship. The unions are pretty well gone now; there's a few, I think there's a couple of the union shops in Rhode Island, but the trade just fell apart with imports and other things that there's not much left of the union. Now there was a time when it was a pretty strong thing, it was a three-year apprenticeship—the first year you got 60 percent of your pay, the second year 80 percent, and the third year 90, then, of course, you started with what a journeyman's listed under. When I came out of the Navy I was going to work in radios. In fact, I did take a couple of courses, but the money was better in the lace trade, and I got married at the time, and a family came along.

The lace trade is complicated. Basically the machine weaves a pre-determined pattern—it does weave, it has the bobbins that cross and tie with the threads. It's quite versatile as far as making different types of lace; really, the limits are only up to what the draftsman can draft for it because you can move the threads anywhere, so you can make practically any pattern. Well, to start out with, the designer is the one who dreams up the pattern, and he puts that on paper, and then the draftsman takes his design and puts it down into numbers that will work on the machine; and then the card puncher punches these cards. You saw them out there. I guess they're cards with holes that fingers go in that makes the threads according to the way the draftsman has determined they should be moved for that pattern. Well, the twist end on my job you take the draft as the draftsman has drafted it, and set the machine up to his specifications, and then keep it going.

The trade has changed little over the years. Even since I've been in the trade the yarns are much the same. When I first started, there were no synthetics that I know of, I don't say they weren't invented, but in the lace trade there was not—we had cotton in the bobbins, and cotton or silk on—boy, that silk, that was something else again. Oh, it would break so awful easy, and was hard on your eyes. Of course we didn't have fluorescent lights when I started, too; they had about a forty watt drop bulb you put down here. It's a wonder everybody didn't go blind. And that silk, it was so thin; about the only way you could see it was to hold the light and see where the show was because you could hardly see the silk. It breaks so easy that it was, oh, it was a headache. But then they got into the synthetics and nylons, the dacrons—they were a big improvement. The same way it was in the bobbins now, it's all nylon and there's no lumps, no bumps, all the same size, and you could get more yards in the bobbins, they go further. That is the biggest improvement.

Tom Beardsley

The Deep River Lace factory, left, is deserted today. It closed its doors in 1990, some nine years after this interview with Arthur Cockayne. The factory was built c.1840, and served the local shipyard. It was later used to manufacture wire and metal novelties and button hooks. It produced lace between 1934 and 1990. Arthur still lives in Deep River, a few hundred yards away from the factory. His British roots are demonstrated by a large Union Jack flag in his front garden.

The Deep River Historical Society has an interesting permanent exhibit, displaying jacquard looms, patterns and lacemakers tools such as "warp brass thread holders" and "jockeys." The factory's speciality was lace for curtains, and it employed between 35 and 50 workers, depending on orders.

IX

Robert Louis Ventulette

Connecticut's diversity of occupations has extended beyond its land boundaries. The sea has provided sustenance as well as livelihood since the first inhabitants arrived. The first Connecticut residents to commercially exploit the ocean's resources were the whalers who departed from New London and sailed the world in search of their prey. Those venturing closer to home have been the commercial fishermen who lived in Stonington and other coastal towns, and plied the offshore waters and fishing banks. Working still closer to shore are the sailors who dragged their nets along oyster beds in the shallow waters off the coast of Bridgeport and Norwalk until well into the twentieth century. These "sail dredgers" are last of the sailors who plied their trade in wind-driven boats.

The following is an interview with oysterman Robert Louis Ventulette; conducted by Philip Thorneycraft Teuscher on March 5, 1988, in Lordship, Stratford, Connecticut.

Philip Teuscher: Maybe you could tell us something about your family.

Robert Ventulette: We were brought up in Bridgeport. My father was a natural growther [oysterman who worked natural ground rather than cultivated oyster beds], and he had the boat the *Beatrice*. And we used to call her the *Dishpan* because after we bought the *J. F. Penny* the fellow that came up from New Jersey and brought her to us, he put the *Beatrice* alongside her and he said, "Looks like a little dishpan." She was 50 foot, the *Penny* was. They nicknamed her "Stupper." My father and my uncle Al and my uncle Aldo, they were oysterers and then they would go off in carpentry when things went slow.

Before my time [c. early 1900s] there used to be a hundred and some boats out there at one time. But when I was out there, there was probably about 30 or so boats.

PT: What member of your family started working on the water?

RV: I believe my father did. He was the oldest boy and they lived right down near the water. I believe my grandfather financed him with a boat, and then he went oystering. I went to eighth grade myself, and then I liked to go with my father on the boat all the time. Then I went to work for him as a deckhand. Ever since I could walk I was with him on the boat. When I started making a living at it was around 1939 or '40. Then I worked there with him up to, I think it was around '40, '41, and the War started and I went into Remington Arms for a while. Then I enlisted into service [the Navy] after that. When we came back out of service in 1945, my brother Murty and I, we took over the *Penny* and we put a new engine in her and put new sails on her. We did about $10,000 worth of work on her. I would run the boat when my father was not on the deck, and my brother was running the *Beatrice*.

PT: What did you do in the off-season, in between the times the beds were—

RV: Well, once I went to work for Hitchcock Gas, another time I went to work for Buckley Fuel.

PT: What was Hitchcock Gas?

RV: They were repairing fishing boats and converting navy boats into fishing boats and repairing engines, and general work.

PT: Where was this? In Bridgeport?

RV: Yeah, it would be on the foot of Pembroke Street. Right now they have a marina over there.

PT: Did it look at the time, when you came out of the Navy, that the natural growth business was going to be good?

RV: Things were a little rough during the War. He couldn't get no help or anything. Things were getting a little rough for him [RV's father] so he sank the *Penny* so she would keep swelled up and everything and wouldn't open up. When we come back out of service we took her and we reconditioned her up again.

PT: Did you do this work, your father and you?

RV: My uncle Al did it for us.

PT: He was a ship carpenter?

RV: No, he was a house carpenter, but he used to repair Atlantic sailboats for all the people in Stamford, Greenwich, and Black Rock [in Bridgeport].He was a good carpenter. He used to have his own little ship yard just for the Atlantics, you know, more of a part-time job. Before my time [c. early 1900s] there used to be a hundred and some boats out there at one time. But when I was out there, there was probably about 30 or so boats.

PT: Why were sail boats used?

RV: Well, because it was against the law to use engines. At one time my father told me, they used to have to take their propellers off and sail them in and out, so they wouldn't use power. Later they let them keep the props on them and they just used sail.

PT: What was the reason for that, basically?

RV: Well, to keep the big companies from coming in and dredging on the natural growthers.

PT: Who administered this?

RV: Well, the Shellfish Commissioners of the State of Connecticut did. You had to buy a license for each man that was on deck. You had to pay a license for your boat.

PT: Was there a season?

RV: Yeah, it would be like from September 20 to July 20.

PT: Why did they have the season not in the summertime?

RV: To give the chance for the oysters to spawn and set. Like with the big companies, they would spread nice clean shells overboard [free-swimming young oysters attach themselves to shells or other material]. And then when the oysters spawned, if they were lucky, they spawned and set where the shells were. Even old boots or glass they would settle on. That's what they would call "seed oysters."

PT: How was the natural ground different from those grounds where they cut down the shells?

RV: Well, we would have to scrape more or less. A company knew just where they put their shells. A lot of times you would

Continued on page 140

Tom Beardsley

Left and below are oyster boats of the Tallmadge Brothers Oyster Company of Norwalk, returning to port and unloading their catch. Connecticut's oyster industry is celebrated each year by the Norwalk Oyster Festival, which takes place during the week after Labor Day.

Oysters were a dietary staple of coastal Indians and pre-Revolutionary Americans. A colonial law to protect oysters was passed as early as 1715. Long Island Sound oyster farmers pioneered the practice of repopulating prime growing grounds with juvenile oysters transplanted from remote, more thickly settled beds. By the start of the 20th century, the industry was in decline because of overfishing. There has been a revival in recent years, and oysters are again being fished on Connecticut's Long Island Sound. Oystermen, like Bridgeport's "natural growther" Robert Ventullete, carried on the state's long tradition during the leaner times.

Tom Beardsley

Norwalk Historical Reference Library

Above and below are black and white reproductions of two Works Progress Administration (WPA) murals depicting Norwalk oystering. They were painted on the walls of Norwalk High School by artist Alexander J. Rummler (1867-1959) during 1937 and 1938. Rummler's 16 murals and 8 panels were commissioned by the Federal Art Project of the WPA in 1936. They were restored during the 1980s, and are now part of a permanent exhibit at Norwalk's City Hall, which is located in the old Norwalk High School. *Mopping For Starfish* (1937), above, is 6 feet 2 inches high and 10 feet long. *Dredging for Oysters* (1938), is 6 feet 2 inches high and 16 feet long.

Norwalk Historical Reference Library

go out there and you'd be working and you wouldn't hit a spot where there was many oysters. You'd just keep looking and checking. Each spot you would try, you'd take a range like on shore. You'd line up a tower with a flagpole or with a building. That way you would know where you were.You know, the water is so funny out there that you wouldn't know. You'd drop a piece here, and you thought it was here, but it was a mile away.

PT: Could you please describe to me what the daily routine would be. What time would you leave home? Did you stay aboard the boat at night?

RV: No. We'd get up and we'd be down at the boat before sunrise, and we'd be out there for sunrise and we'd work until sunset.

PT: What was the highest wind condition you could work in?.

RV: Well, we'd try not to work when it would start to blow to darn hard. Starting in up there at 12 knots or that, we would either reef in [tie down the sails] or say, "To heck with it," and call it a day.

PT: What was the reason for this?

RV: Well, it was hard working, you know, standing on deck and you'd be pounding around. Now, see the *Penny*, we used to have winders on her. We'd have two dredges on her, one on each side of the boat [the dredge was a metal frame used to harvest oysters by dragging it along the oyster bed; the "winder" was a winding machine that lowered and raised the dredge]. We would sail her up and down the Sound, where with the *Dishpan*, we would pull five dredges but you could only go with the wind and the tide, and then you'd have to come back on a drift.

PT: What was the shortest drift that you could make that wouldn't be a hassle for you? Would it be a quarter of a mile or a couple hundred feet?

RV: Well, with sailing the boat, sometimes you'd go maybe a thousand feet or so. If oystering was good you would haul and heave, which I mean is you'd get your dredges up and just when you'd get them empty and everything was square, you'd let them right back over again and you'd make a long drift.

PT: When could you tell that the dredge was about ready to be pulled, if you were on a long drift? What would you feel?

RV: Well, it was more or less your timing. You'd jest figure how long it would be. There was not a way of grabbing the dredge and saying. It was more or less your knowledge of how long you should pull it. It would be like a fisherman. He goes out and he says he'd be pulling his net for an hour and a half, and after an hour and a half he'd have nothing in it.

PT: Experience.

RV: Yeah.

PT: And when you pulled the dredge, what would you say it weighed?

RV: Well, they were pretty heavy. One day I was working on the *Beatrice* with my father and his crew. I was pulling the dredges and I was only a young man, and I just got mine up to the break of the water, and I said to him, "I think I strained my milk". The dredge was so heavy, and they started laughing and they dropped their wedges all back down again. So that meant they had to pull theirs up again! But they never did forget it, you know. Some of them dredges were a couple of hundred pounds.

PT: What about your boats?

RV: Well, the *Dishpan*, she was a good working boat. One day I was out there and we were working the harbor that time, Bridgeport Harbor. We were getting near the lighthouse and we were coming back on the drift, when all of a sudden I got a knock down. A "knock down" is, if you're not watching your boat when you're in the wind, and you get a puff of wind, she'll take your boat right onto her side, and if you're not careful you'll be sunk. Well, that's what happened. I went over and I was standing in water up to my knees.

PT: On the bottom?

RV: No, in the boat. The decks were under about a foot, and I hollered to my brother-in-law, he was my deck hand. I hollered to him, "Let the jib [sail] go and drop the peak." He said, "To hell with you! I'm hanging on!".

It's always nice out there oystering. A lot of times you'd pray for rain or the wind to come up because you were getting tired. Like I say, sunrise to sunset, they were long days. We used to have some good times out there. Another time the old man got—the guys, they were all older than I was. I was only a kid then. They brought a bottle aboard the boat. We were doing good; we were really catching oysters. All of a sudden I could see that something's wrong. We are not doing good. I look back and my father's stiffer than heck at the wheel. Well, we were paying off $10,000 then, my brother and I. So I come up on the deck and I went up to them and I says to them, " If I find out which one of you son of a bitches brought aboard that bottle, I'll kill you. I'll take you down one at a time, right now!"

I had to finish working the boat that day. So then we were on our way in and the engine wasn't running in the *Dishpan* so we went over to give my brother—he was running the *Dishpan* then—gave him a line and had him towing behind us. We were coming into the harbor and my father come staggering out of the aftercabin, and he says to me, "I'll take over the boat." And I says, "Watch where the hell you're going. You'll have her aground in two minutes." I no sooner said it and we hit! The *Penny* took five feet of water and the *Dishpan* only about a foot and a half. Well, I had to holler to my brother, "Unsnap the line in a hurry." He flew by me. I said to my father, "Get into that son of a bitch of a rowboat before I kill you." I had to stay there for four hours 'til the tide dropped and came back up again! And then I had to take the ribbing besides. All the other oystermen coming in, you know, and I'm on the sand bar! As I say, those are memories. Some are good and some aren't.

X

Mabel Batts

In the 1920s and 1930s, several dozen shirt and dress making shops were established in New Haven by factory owners from New York City, who wanted to avoid the costs of wage increases and improved safety standards won by such garment workers unions as the Amalgamated Clothing Workers of America (ACWA), for shirtmakers, and the International Ladies Garment Workers Union (ILGWU), for dressmakers. In New Haven, 80 percent of the garment workers were women, a majority of them Italian. Often first-generation Italian-American teenagers worked side-by-side with their Italian-born mothers. In addition, Polish, Irish and Jewish young women, along with members of other ethnic groups, worked in the shops as well. Among them was a small, but growing number of African-Americans.

In 1932 and 1933, hundreds of these women, from several dozen shirt and dress shops in New Haven, banded together to put an end to "sweatshop" conditions. [The term "sweat shop" was used by the Manufacturers Association of Connecticut in 1933 to describe the deplorable conditions of New Haven's garment industry.] They were eventually successful in gaining recognition for chapters, or "locals," of both the ACWA and the ILGWU.

Mabel Batts was one of these women. Born in New Haven, she went to work in a shirt factory at age 18, and continued in the industry for over 60 years. When the union struck Lesnow's shirt factory in 1933, she helped convince her sister workers to "stick to the union." After the union's victory, she was elected the first African-American union officer for the Amalgamated Clothing Workers Union in New England. She was interviewed by Steven Lassonde for the Greater New Haven Labor History Project on September 29, 1989.

Mabel Batts: I was born December 5, 1909 in New Haven, Connecticut. I am the fifth generation in New Haven, on the women's side.

In the 1930s and 1940s, there was nothing else for a woman to do. If you were a high school graduate, you were supposed to be smart. But still, there was nothing for you to do.

Steve Lassonde: You have lived in New Haven all your life?

MB: No. Between the age of 7 and fourteen, I went to Montclair, New Jersey, and I lived there with my father and my grandmother. And I was very lucky [growing up there, in a neighborhood with many Italian families] to learn how to speak Italian.

SL: What did your father do for a living?

MB: He was a horse and buggy man, a carriage driver, until the carriage went out. Then he became a taxi driver.

SL: So, you came back to New Haven in 1921 or 22?

MB: Right, Then I stayed there for a while. My mother and my stepfather moved to Jersey City when I was fifteen. I went to live with them. My mother's mother got sick when I was sixteen years old, and she came back to New Haven. Between that time I was staying with my stepfather. My family thought I should come back home, and I wanted to stay in Jersey City, so I got married, at 16. I was married only nine months when I came back home to New Haven, with two lovely black eyes. And, of course, my mother was quite upset.

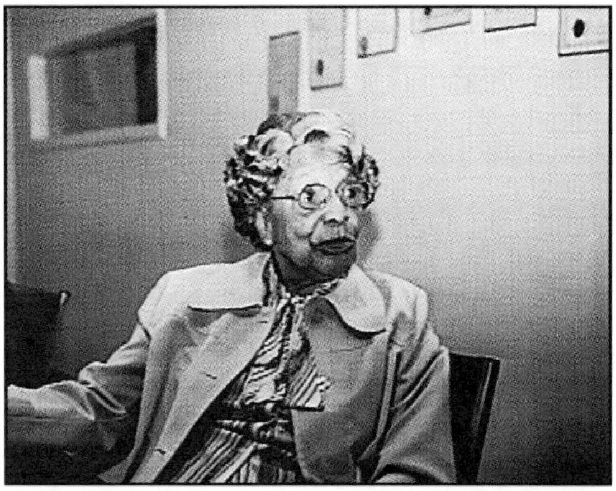

Mabel Batts, as she appeared on a 1991 video entitled, *The Work We've Done: The Contributions of Connecticut's Older Citizens to the Economy of the Nutmeg State.* The tape was produced by the Connecticut State Department on Aging, in conjunction withthe Urban League of Greater Hartford.

My grandmother died in October of 1926. My mother died two years later, on the same day as her mother, October 26, 1928. She was 39. I was 18. In 1927, I went to work in the shirt factory in New Haven, the day after Labor Day, in Lesnow's Shirt Factory. I worked there until it closed, which was either 1938 or 1939. In the meantime, in 1933, we joined the union. We were getting seven cents a dozen for pressing shirts. That's a complete shirt—pinning, folding and everything.

SL: How long would it take you to press one shirt?

MB: You press the cuffs and the collars first. Then you button it up and lay it out flat, as neat as possible. Then, in those days, when I went to work in the shirt factory, it was mostly men. And they used to use their knees to hold the shirt down to press it on the table. But, of course, being women, we couldn't do that. So, what they did was give us a brick, covered up with cloth, and we used to use a spray gun. I don't know if you've ever seen a spray gun they used to kill the flies with?

SL: Oh, sure.

MB: That's what we used to wet the shirts to press them. Our iron weighed over twenty-five pounds. It was like an oven. You would take it and light it with a match. My average was three dozen shirts in an hour, at least. The highest I ever pressed was twenty-six dozen a day. But I couldn't do that every day.

SL: So, that would be about $1. 75 a day?

MB: But don't forget, that wouldn't be every day. I couldn't keep up that pace. The highest I think I ever averaged was about six dollars a week. When we go in—we were supposed to start at eight o'clock, but we never did. We started before. Whatever time you got to work, the iron was already hot. And I was one who liked to get to work a little early so I could get my pins, my tissue paper, my cardboard. We used to have to number our cardboards on our shirts, to let them know who did the shirts.

I'd get there about seven-thirty, and work until five-thirty, and take about—it's supposed to be about a half-hour for lunch, but we'd always be less, because we wanted to make the money. It was piecework [pay for each shirt pressed, rather than by the hour]—the five minutes you lost was lost.

Then on Saturdays—this is something I always brag about, I don't know why—I used to get fired most every Saturday. Our boss had a son who was very uncouth. At twelve o'clock we're supposed to stop. And he'd come, and "Oh, I got six more shirts for you to do. I got six more shirts." So, by the time we got the six shirts done each time, it would be at least one-thirty or two o'clock before we'd get through. So, therefore, I would get angry. After I caught on to what he was doing, I would stop, and he'd say to me, "I said, do six more shirts." And, of course, I had a very big mouth, and I said, "No. Abraham Lincoln freed the slaves." And he says, "I'm the boss." And I'd tell him to take his job and shove it. And I'd get fired, and as I'm going out the door, his uncle would say, "Mabel, don't forget to be back Monday morning." That would go on.

Then one time I got angry, and I said to the uncle, "I'm not coming back any more." It happened that I was a good presser, a fast presser, so therefore I knew I didn't have to worry about a job. I went to work in another shirt factory for about two weeks. Then he'd call me to go back, and I'd come back, and work again.

In 1931, at the height of the Depression, I was making no money. I got mad at my boss again, and went to work in another shirt factory. It was called the D and I Shirt Factory. That was on View Street. I lived with my aunt on Grand and South Front Street. I used to walk all the way from South Front Street to View Street every morning, 'cause I didn't have money. I gave her three dollars a week, but then I didn't have lunch half the time. That left me with about a dollar and a half or two dollars a week.

I met my second husband in 1932, the year we had the strike at Lesnow. There was a store on Collis Street, right across from Lesnow's, and we used to buy our lunch there. And when we had a strike, Harry Lesnow, dear old soul, went over there and told him not to let us come in and keep warm. And he didn't let us come in any more. And the union had told us that if anyone was going to get arrested, for us to crowd them, so they could escape. So, one of my friends—we're still friends to this day—the cop was going to arrest her, and she jumped up on his back. She was only about four-foot ten, and she jumped up on his back. And we all had to start laughing, 'cause she was hanging on his back. Anyway, she didn't get arrested. We were on strike a long time.

SL: What precipitated the strike?

MB: Seven cents a dozen. That is, the pressers were being paid only seven cents for every dozen shirts they pressed. Then the union came and it was trying to organize us—the Amalgamated Clothing Workers of America. We joined—I got my first union card in May, 1933. Lesnow's had over sixty pressers. I became chair lady of the pressing department. I was very proud, for I was a minority in the shirt factory.

SL: One of five blacks in the shirt factory?

MB: At the time when I went in. But when I became chair lady, there must have been about eight or nine in the pressing department. In the sewing room, if there were two in the whole building, it was a miracle.

SL: What did the union at Lesnow's accomplish?

MB: The piece rate went up quite a bit. Then we worked 40 hours a week, down from 50 hours. Saturdays were eliminated. Also, we had our health insurance and our holiday pay, which we never had had. I used to take weeks off in the summertime, because I couldn't stand the heat. But, I didn't get paid for it. We didn't have any sick benefits before the union.

Lesnow's went out of business. Then Brewster's came from Danbury, Connecticut, into the same building where Lesnow's was, and I went there to work, and I was also chairlady of the pressing department. And I worked there until they went out of business. [Women garment workers were mostly young, but sometimes members of more than one generation in the same family worked together.] I know some girls whose mothers worked there.

SL: As far as you know, did the younger women work there before they got married, and had children, and then they would come back to work after they had kids and the kids were in school?

MB: Yes. They had a nursery in the Brewster Shirt Factory, for the women who worked. First, it used to be the women who would take care of the children. The manager of Brewsters Shirt Factory let women go for an hour to take care of the kids when they came out of school. Then he went and hired someone after it got bigger, just to come there and take care of the kids, which was very good. He was one of the nicest bosses I ever worked for.

SL: Was there anything unusual about your work experience during the war? Did the labor force change at all?

MB: Yes. A lot of women left the shirt factory.

SL: For higher paying jobs?

MB: Right. I stayed in the shirt factory, I never made a lot of money. But I also liked my job. And for someone who was going to stay a short time! I had a cousin who went to work with me at the same time. She stayed three days, and I stayed 48 years. I'm the first person in our local to retire after 48 years of working.

SL: Who remained in the factory where you worked?

MB. The older women. In the 1930s and 1940s, there was nothing else for a woman to do. If you were a high school graduate, you were supposed to be smart. But still, there was nothing for you to do.

SL: Clerical work began to open up, didn't it?

I never made a lot of money. But I also liked my job. And for someone who was going to stay a short time! I had a cousin who went to work with me at the same time. She stayed three days, and I stayed 48 years. I'm the first person in our local to retire after 48 years of working.

MB: Not until the late 1940s. But you had all those other years. And then they weren't getting much. They had the prestige of the job, but they weren't making a lot of money. When I went to work in the shirt factory, most of the women I knew were doing domestic work. In fact, I don't know anybody else who was close to me that worked in the factory. As far as they were concerned, that was a let down. I was supposed to be shamed—to think that I worked in the factory! It had a very bad name—working in the shirt factory. They would try to embarrass me, and I would say, on Thursdays I get a paycheck.

I'm not educated, and one of the younger generation would say to me, don't you feel bad? Look at you, you stayed in the shirt factory. And I said, well I wasn't qualified to do anything else. And it was an honest living. That why I tell you young people to go to school and be qualified to do something.

XI

Stanley Jackson Sumner

The following Connecticut native never labored in a mill or a factory, though he occasionally worked on a farm. He was from an upper class farming family whose patriarch decided to move from rural Connecticut into an urban area to pursue a career in business. The Sumners were a self-described old Yankee family, the descendants of British immigrants who had arrived in Connecticut in the 18th century. The urban area the Sumners chose was Willimantic, which, in the early years of the century was a thriving textile city, offering plenty of opportunities for an ambitious entrepreneur. He was interviewed by Tom Beardsley, March 15, 1993, for the Windham Textile & History Museum's Oral History Archive.

I was born in Eastford, Connecticut on March 6, 1902 . We lived on a farm belonging to my father's family. When I was a year old he swapped with a cousin whose father, Mr. Warren, ran the Eastford country store. My father wanted to get off the farm and they made some kind of a deal. My father ended up in the store and Mr. Warren wound up on the farm.

(The house) must have been very costly to build. The woodwork was all cherry downstairs and each bedroom upstairs had a marble wash bowl and running water and so forth. There was a big sitting room downstairs and a front parlor. A big dining room paneled in oak, and, of course, in the kitchen they had a pantry between the kitchen and dining room and laundry, and a butler's place.

My father's name was Edwin Otis Sumner. The Sumners are an old Yankee family. They came to the Eastford area, which was Ashford then, later divided into Eastford and Ashford, somewhere in the early 1700s. They came to Dorchester or Roxbury, I've forgotten which, around Boston in 1636. They came from Bicester, near Oxford in England. The family were farmers for several generations. I don't know exactly but my father had quite a big acreage in Eastford. I had a brother, Homer, who died in 1964 of a stroke, he was five years younger than I. My mother's maiden name was Eva Jackson. The Jacksons have lived in Woodstock for many years, from the 1700s sometime. They came from England too, settling up near Boston somewhere, I can't remember the name of the town, my son Jackson has the genealogy telling exactly. They are Yankees way back. The Sumners came down from two brothers who came over, one was George and one was William.

I didn't really live on the farm, being about a year old when they moved down to the village and my father ran the store. That went on until I was about six years old, and then they moved to Willimantic in 1908. We lived up on Summit Street. Then it was just one street over from the woods on the edge of town. As kids we played in the woods and grew up that way. We always had a cow or two and had a big garden and raised potatoes and things. My grandfather would buy a half of a hog that somebody butchered and bring it home—and my grandmother made ham and bacon and sausage and things like that, and that went on as long as she lived.

I'm not sure why the family moved to Willimantic. I think they looked at Putnam and Webster and decided that Willimantic was the best place to go. I think one thing that they were thinking of was the educational facilities for my brother and me, and the fact that the railroad was there and transportation was better. At the time my grandfather, Frank Jackson, and father were cutting off wood lots—they didn't own a saw mill but had arrangements with a man who did. They would buy the lots, get somebody to cut the timber and have the mill saw it and my grandfather would sell the lumber. They were in business as lumber merchants, calling themselves Jackson and Sumner. They went to Boston and Providence frequently, places like that, to sell mostly pine—boxboards and things that the pine was used for.

My father did a number of things in Willimantic. For a while they ran a little woodworking plant in South Windham and made pick 'o sticks and axe handles and things of that nature. Pick 'o sticks went into the cotton mills, but I don't know exactly what they did. That wasn't very profitable and they gave it up. My father then got the job as superintendent of streets and of public works in Willimantic. He did that for two or three years. In the meantime they bought a half interest in a clothing store in Willimantic and ran that.

My middle name is Jackson, after my mother, who looked after the house. She never worked. My grandfather was the one who was the business end of the family, more than my father, and as I recall it, the house at 183 Summit Street and the house across the street, 194 North Street, had been foreclosed and someone had a mortgage on both of them. My grandfather made some kind of a deal with whoever had taken over the mortgages and Mr. Hurley—he was later in the Hurley-Grant Company (a well - known hardware store in Willimantic)—and my grandfather had some arrangement so that if my grandfather bought both of them he'd take one of them off his hands which he did, so that the Hurleys lived there about the time we did, on the other corner of Summit and North.

Our house was originally Colonel Joseph Dwight Chaffee's house. Chaffee was a well known Willimantic silk manufacturer [President of the Natchaug Silk Company, 1889-1895, which manufactured dress silks, and the Chaffee Manufacturing Company, 1900-1927, which produced fish lines.] When we moved in the house was empty, I suppose it stood there waiting for someone to buy it. I don't think anyone lived there between the time the Chaffees moved out and we moved in. My folks went there in 1908 and my brother Homer sold it in 1953, I think. It must have been very costly to build. The woodwork was all cherry downstairs and each bedroom upstairs had a marble wash bowl and running water and so forth. There was a big sitting room downstairs and a front parlor. A big dining room paneled in oak, and, of course, in the kitchen they had a pantry between the kitchen and dining room and laundry, and a butler's place, I guess. Of course, my family never had any help of that kind, but it was all there and Chaffee had set it up to live in great style.

Tom Beardsley

The house in which Stanley lived as a young boy was built in 1889 by Willimantic's leading silk manufacturer, Joseph Dwight Chaffee. It is one of many fine Victorian mansions located in the city's hill district.

When we moved in there was, in addition to my father, mother, brother, grandfather Jackson, and his wife, my great grandmother—my grandmother Jackson's mother—and my father's mother—who had originally been Sarah Jane Hanks. So, we had quite a family in the house but there was plenty of room and we didn't have to get under each other's feet. There, were, let's see, one, two, three, four, five. I guess there were five bedrooms, but there were a couple of rooms that had been bedrooms which they made into a little kitchen and dining room for my grandfather Jackson and his wife, like a small apartment. The weather vane on the top of the house—we used to pepper it with BB shots and air rifles when we could hit it. It has the letter C in it, for Chaffee.

Grandfather Jackson had started on a farm in Woodstock and got into the native lumber business, carrying on in that until about 1921. In the meantime, he'd been in politics, in the Connecticut Legislature, the Connecticut Senate, from Woodstock. After being in Willimantic for a while he also went into the automobile business and they had a garage and sold Overland cars and

Chevrolets for a while, and Willis Knights. They must have bought that around 1915, continuing until about 1925.

I went to high school in Willimantic, and Phillips Exeter for a little while in the fall of 1918. And then the flu came and my mother was frightened and wanted me to come home so I went home for two or three weeks. When I went back they told me I'd have to go to summer school to catch up, and I got into an argument with them and walked out, and came back to high school. I didn't lose any time. Phillips Exeter is a preparatory school in New Hampshire and still is a top notch school. They told me I'd have to lose a year or go to summer school, and I said I wasn't going to. I came back and worked in high school—I'd found out how to work while I was up there—and got into Yale without any trouble.

I graduated in 1920. At Yale, I majored in history and economics. I liked history, but I hadn't any career plans. I thought about teaching history, but I tried the automobile business and didn't like it so I went into the insurance business with Mr. George Elliot, who was a much older man, and that's where I stayed.

Willimantic was quite a prosperous little community. The streets were always busy. We had good times as kids growing up—did things in the Boy Scouts, and in the school with football, basketball, and all of that. It was a good place to live and there were a lot of young fellows about my age. Where we lived I guess there were nine or ten boys about my age around just one or two squares there. That was pretty busy!

The families in Willimantic were from different stock—the Hurleys and the Raffertys were Irish, and were close friends of mine. Bray Rafferty grew up to become a surgeon and practiced here and Bob, his brother was a dentist and also practiced here. There were several ethnic groups other than the Irish—French, of course, who lived down in the lower end of town and there were some Italians up where the little park is, the West End it was called. There were Swedes. The Lutheran Church at the junction of Summit and Oak Street was built for Swedish people who lived in that area. There were a few Syrians who lived down around Milk Street. Sabos and, let me think, oh, Haddads—there were always Haddads. A very few Jewish families, the Rosens, Israels and Hotchbergs.

There were many silk and cotton mills in town then. I remember a big strike at the American Thread cotton mills in 1925—about a year after I got out of college. There was trouble going all the time down there because they called the police in and they were importing what they called scabs. A neighbor of ours, May Smith had worked down there in the inspecting room for years. She refused to go out on the strike, and used to cross the picket lines every day. They threatened her but never did anything to her. I don't remember anything very definite about the strike, but the general feeling among people was that they didn't care much about unions, thought they were trouble makers. I presume if they supported anyone it would have been the company. I don't seem to remember seeing any of the marches. We didn't live near the center of town so weren't apt to see them. We knew they were going on but that was about it.

I never worked in the textile mills. Most of the kids I grew up with at some time or other went to work in the mills during the summer and one or two went to work there permanently. But I never had any desire to work in a mill. With the sort of farm background I had, with my folks keeping a cow and a horse, and having a big garden, and other things, I was used to that kind of outside work, so when I got jobs I worked up at Stearns, Mountain Dairy in Mansfield, on Saturdays, during vacations and in winter, like Christmas vacations and days off. Then later I worked down in Rhode Island three summers on a farm while I was in college, so the work I was used to doing was farm work.

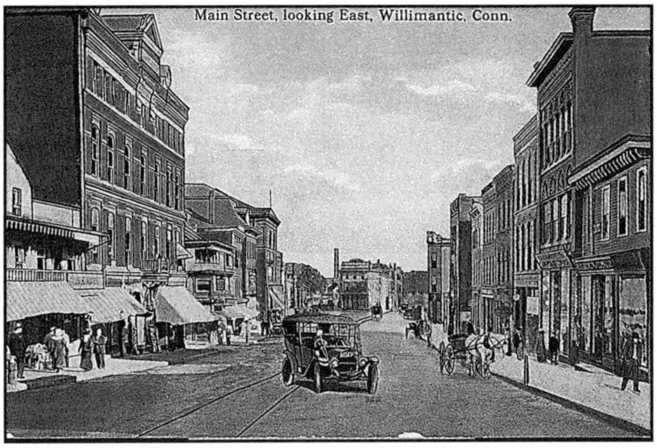

Windham Textile & History Museum

The Willimantic of Stanley Sumner's youth, a busy cotton and silk producing community, and a very important railroad center in the northeast corridor.

When I got back from Yale I went into the automobile business with my folks for a couple of years, in car sales. I didn't like it and decided to do something else. My grandfather suggested I see George Elliott, a local insurance broker, because he knew him well. I went down to see him one day and asked him if he'd be interested in selling out a interest in the business, which was insurance. We worked out something finally and it worked very well. We actually founded the partnership in January 1927. Mr. Elliott stayed on until about 1940. In the meantime, my brother, Homer, had come along and was working there. My brother bought Mr. Elliot's share and that's how the firm became known as Sumner and Sumner. We hired a fellow named Bill Thompson and he was with us until he retired, and then Jackson came along. He was in the navy between World War II and the

Vietnam War. He bought Homer's interest, after his Uncle Homer had died. His full name is Jackson Peale Sumner, Peale was his mother's name. He runs the firm now. I've been involved with the business for more than sixty years, and for many years I was also involved with The Willimantic Chamber of Commerce.

Stanley Sumner died after a short illness in April, 1994, aged 92.

Olan Mills

Stanley Sumner, pictured in 1988, aged 86, and still actively involved in the Sumner & Sumner Insurance Company

XII

Laura Knott Twine

To the stories of Connecticut's myriad occupations must be added the stories of those who have labored to document and preserve the history of work. One such remarkable story is that of Laura Knott Twine. Born to a working-class family, she overcame a number of economic and social disadvantages, and eventually founded the Windham Textile and History Museum, in Willimantic. Laura talks about her youth in East Hartford, ethnicity, religious discovery, work and the formation of the museum. Interview, conducted July 10, 1993, by Tom Beardsley.

I was born Laura Mae Knott in St. Francis Hospital in Hartford, on November 11, 1946. My father was born in Springfield, Massachusetts in 1914. My mother was born in Hartford in 1915. She is from the Goodwin clan, one of the founding groups of Hartford. My mother was the 11th consecutive generation of Goodwins to be born there.

Whatever happens in the future, we have all done a great deal of work to preserve much of the history of this section of Eastern Connecticut. So none of the effort has been wasted.

My mother and father met in Hartford, but my mother had a difficult time getting her family to accept my father. He was orphaned young, and was partly raised through the Salvation Army. He left school when he was only 14. My Dad was from old Yankee stock too. His mother was an Avery, the clan which founded New London. It was really important to him, and he pursued the family genealogy, and I took it over when I was about 20. He was employed at Pratt & Whitney.

I am the youngest of five children, four girls and a boy. When I was born, my parents had recently purchased one of those post-war houses, built row after row, in East Hartford. My mother worked at a variety of jobs. She was a sales clerk at Robert Hall Clothes up on Route 5 in East Hartford, and also worked at the JB Soap Factory on the line. The kids looked after themselves while my parents were working. I never remember a baby-sitter. It was convenient to have a mother who worked if you did not like school. I often skipped school, starting in the sixth grade. I remember once heating chicken soup, and while watching "I Love Lucy" on TV, I burned the soup and had to air out the house before anyone came home, so I would not get caught!

Tom Beardsley

Laura Knott Twine poses outside the museum she founded in the mid 1980s. The Windham Textile and History Museum officially opened in September,1989. It occupies two buildings, erected in 1877, which served as provision stores for workers employed at the Willimantic Linen Company. The vast mills of that company can be seen in the background.

The Willimantic Linen Company (1854-1898) manufactured high quality cotton thread. It was taken over in 1898 by a British organization, the American Thread Company, which produced cotton and synthetic textiles in the city until 1985. At its height, in 1916/17, the company employed more than 3,000 workers in the Willimantic mills.

I was brought up in what could be typically called a working-class area on Bedford Avenue in East Hartford. It was a neighborhood consisting of many Italian-Americans. We were one of the few Protestant families in the neighborhood. My parents were not particularly religious. I was baptized in a Congregational church, but a few years later my mother became involved in the Methodist church. I often went to church without my parents, and by the time I was in the sixth and seventh grade, I had developed a strong attraction to the Catholic faith. Indeed, most of my schoolfriends were Catholics. Also, when I was four, I had a serious kidney disease and spent a long time in St. Francis Hospital, and remember the nuns being extremely kind—so that was my first comfort factor with the Catholic church.

I recall many of the families that lived in East Hartford in the 1950s, the Lucianos and the Diglianis, and a black woman from Jamaica. My best friend was called Maria Andronica. When her parents became citizens, they changed her name to Mary Ann. It was a shame to lose such a nice name. The experience of all different kind of foods, and their smells, is a very strong memory of that neighborhood—and there were hundreds of kids. I also recall a Jewish family, but I never really met any black kids until the seventh or eighth grades. At school we had these regional dances, and the black kids from the projects came to our dances, and were also be on the various sports teams. As I recall, there was never any prejudice or trouble among the children.

It was not a "Donna Reed" type neighborhood. It had its social problems. It was not a wealthy area by any means, but some of the families were a little better off than us. We had a round screen black and white TV, but one of the families had a color TV. This was sometime around 1956 or 1957. Also at that time, a new housing development was built nearby, and all the kids who came to live there, came to our school. Their parents were management people at "Pratt"—no one ever said "Pratt & Whitney"— so these kids came to school with really nice clothes.

My father never owned a car until 1960, when he bought a 1955 Ford Fairlane, which we loved. Before then he walked three miles to work every day. My father and mother always worked. There was plenty of employment in the 1950s. I suppose the late

1950s were my "Happy Days." I remember a day trip to Springfield, Massachusetts on the train. My father took three of us kids. We had a great time at Riverside Park, but we missed the train home! My parents did not have a telephone, so he couldn't let my mother know. To placate us as we waited for the next train he gave us a couple of quarters and we made a record for my mother, which I still have. My brother sounds just like "Fonzy," and I have what sounds like a strong Brooklyn accent!

I guess I had a normal childhood for the neighborhood I grew up in. I went to Hockanum school from kindergarten to the eighth grade. I hated school. I cried everyday in the fourth grade, and I left school not being able to read or write very well. In my Freshman year I only attended on 23 days. I went to East Hartford high school, signed in and went off for the day, and returned to sign out.

At 13 I started dating my future husband, and by the time I was 15, I was pregnant. I remember thinking, "that's not going to happen to me!" But my elder sister was pregnant at 16, and my brother got his girlfriend pregnant. And my other sister was also expecting a child, so four of the five Knott children were all pregnant before they were 20 years old.

My mother, my boyfriend's mother and my boyfriend and I drove to Dillon, South Carolina—a state which allowed minors to be married. We drove down in a 1956 Ford, with the doors wired shut, with a screwdriver for a shift handle and a rope on the clutch pedal to pull it back up! We got married then drove back home. We moved in with his parents, into the basement of his house in Glastonbury. My son was born in a blizzard in 1963, and within a year we had moved into the projects in East Hartford. We then moved into a small house in Marlborough, and had a daughter in 1966. We split up in 1969. I stayed in the house. I didn't have a job, I had no money, I had no education, I had no high school diploma—but I had two young children to support, so I went onto welfare for about a year, and later got a job at a day care center.

I met my husband, Richard Twine in 1968, and he encouraged me to go and get my high school diploma. He introduced me to a lot of different reading material—and I just read and read and read, so I only really started to read when I was aged 20. Richard was recently separated, and had two children. We married in 1973 and moved into his house, sold my house and I paid back my welfare bill. Richard was born in England, and he came to live in the United States in 1967 after serving in the Royal Navy. He was employed at Colts as an engineer and a designer. We were married when I was 26, and had four children under the age of ten—two of mine and two of his.

I took the GED test to get my high school diploma at Manchester Community College. The moderator called me up and asked me what I was going to do, as I had passed the GED well. He wanted me to continue my education, but I just laughed. I had little money and two babies to support. But the moderator managed to get me a scholarship for a year, and I took early childhood education classes, thinking this would get me ahead in the day care system. However, the center closed, but I was licensed by this time, and I took eleven children into my house in Marlborough. I did that for two years, and also worked as a volunteer teacher's aide for a while at Elmer Theines school. I was then employed at Gilead Hill school and taught a special education classes there. It was remedial reading on the third and fourth grade level, which was just about where I got stuck, so it was kind of fun to help the kids.

We took the four kids on a church camp outing for three weeks to Prince Edward Island and New Brunswick with 11 other families. We went to a place called King's Landing. People actually live in the houses and barter, and raise the corn and eat it, so it is truly a living museum. I became very interested in the weaving I saw there. I had seen weaving being done once before at Sturbridge Village, when I was in the eighth grade, and became interested in it there, so Kings Landing renewed my interest.

I said to myself then, before I am 50 years old. I am going to do two things. I am going to learn how to do this weaving stuff, and I am going to learn how to ride a horse! I achieved the former, but I never did learn how to ride a horse. I took weaving lessons with Kate Edgerton, who was a tremendous teacher with great character. She was an enabler. She guided my life and made me think about what I was going to do when all the kids left home, and she encouraged me to teach weaving. I subsequently opened my own weaving shop by 1980, and I took over Kate Edgerton's business after she retired.

Today, thousands of local people are still connected to the old mills because their families originally came here to work in them. This is a museum which belongs to the community.

Richard and I moved into a bigger house in Windham in 1978, and I became more aware of the textile industry. There was a lot of talk at the time of the textile industry closing. I thought that at some point colonial people moved into the factory and continued weaving to create cloth, but I soon found out that was the furthest thing from the truth. Colonial type spinning and weaving continued right up until the 1890s. A lot of the hand looms of New England were packed onto wagons and went west with the pioneers, but the people left behind in the East were buying clothes off the racks in the shops, and taking advantage of machine-made textiles, and the people who worked in those textile mills were not the old weavers and spinners, but mainly made up of the migrants and immigrants who came during the industrial revolution.

I joined the Windham Historical Society and discussed the fact that Willimantic was a mill town, and that its multiculturism was reflected in the vast array of churches and social clubs here. The Society tended to focus more upon Windham Center and the founding of the town, but I felt more should be done to look at the industrial history, and at working class people, so the seed for the Windham Textile & History Museum was sown. I set out to collect information about the local history, but there was very little information about the generations of people who had worked in the local mills. Today, thousands of local people are still connected to the old mills because their families originally came here to work in them. This is a museum which belongs to the community.

I suppose this museum started in 1984, when I heard that Willimantic's American Thread Company had space to preserve some of its history. I met with the president of the American Thread Company, along with a history professor from Eastern Connecticut State University, David Roth, and we discussed the viability of creating a museum. I wrote a paper about the importance of preserving the history of the working people, and elevating its importance into the community's mind. I was really set on the idea, and was determined to see it through. I picked up a book at a tag sale put out by the American Association of State and Local History about American museums. In it was a long check list of things you had to have to say you were a museum, and I used it as my bible, and sought out expert people in the field.

Unfortunately, the American Thread Company decided not to donate any space or property for preservation or a museum. I was somewhat annoyed, as I had already organized a board of directors. I discussed the problem with them, and we decided to continue to collect material and promote the idea of a museum. We waited for the American Thread Company to sell out. Once they moved from Willimantic, we made a bid for some property from the new owners. A lady called Harriet Ledgerwood, the great granddaughter of Austin Cornelius Dunham, the founder of the American Thread Company—then known as the Willimantic Linen Company—was the next door neighbor of Jonathan Dugan, the new owner of the mill site. She convinced him of the need for a museum, and he donated the buildings to us. He was a great benefactor, and a very nice man. And I must say that there have been a great number of benefactors to this museum over the years. The number is probably close to 600.

Whatever happens in the future, we have all done a great deal of work to preserve much of the history of this section of Eastern Connecticut. So none of the effort has been wasted.

XIII

Charles H. Johnson

A Hartford resident born in Louisville, Kentucky, in 1892, Charles H. Johnson tells a very different story of enterprise in the Nutmeg State. From cooper [barrelmaker] to porter to independent entrepreneur, his working life has both mirrored and defied the typical picture of the black experience in this country.

Among the unexpected associations Johnson has maintained is his long-time membership in an African-American lodge of Masons—a service organization with elaborate rituals based on a secret fraternal order founded in England in the early 1700s, with roots in the practices of medieval stonemasons' trade guilds. Masons have been active here since the American Revolution, although the first black Masons lodge wasn't formed until the 1800s. The housing project where Mr. Johnson resided, in Hartford's predominantly Black north end, was built by the Tuscan Brotherhood, a local African-American Masonic lodge.

Mr. Johnson also mentions mentions the Louis-Schmelling fight, an important event for those in the African-American community. Joe Louis—viewed not only as a hero of the Black community in his day, but also a symbol of western democracy—defeated his opponent—who had come to represent rising fascism in Germany—in a single round. He was interviewed by David Shuldiner on January 21, 1988, for the program "An Active Age," broadcast on Hartford Community Television.

After ninety some odd years I've put a value on what I've tried to do down through the years, and it has proven to be very, very wonderful, and I am happy and privileged to have lived to see this day. I remember when I was in Louisville, Kentucky, I was living in a different world than what I am living in today. Everything was different. We didn't have airplanes like we have today. I saw the first airplane when they first came into being. I saw the one they tried to put up but couldn't put up. But I finally stayed 'til they got it perfected. Today—you know the story. And when you stop to think that it used to take six months to go across the sea—you go across [now] in six hours. As a matter of fact, since I left Louisville, Kentucky, I've gone in six countries in six hours. That's how the world has changed.

At the time Joe Louis had the fight with Max Schmelling and knocked him out that night in New York City 'round about '37—I was there that night. And it was so fast I didn't even get to see the fight. When I looked up it was all over with.

We used to have horse and buggies at the railroad station, where we use taxi cabs today. And the homes were very well blessed if they had a bicycle. And the other mode of transportation was a wagon and a mule. When I came to Hartford, they still had some of the trolley tracks down.

Back in Kentucky, my family was poor, they had just ordinary work on the farm—hard physical work, that's all we knew about in those days. We were able to go to school—what time we went—we didn't have much time to go. But we did go to school. We did well with the time we had, we accomplished something. We had that desire that Martin Luther King talked about years later—to be somebody, and that was down in our soul, that's what we wanted to be, and in order to be somebody we know we had to do something, to give something. We worked for it, we tried, we did anything we could to get some kind of an education. We got some, and we made the most of what we had.

The first job I had was working in a cooper shop—making barrels. I was just a young boy then. Then I went from that to become a porter on the railroad—Pullman service, out of Kentucky. I served in the Pullman service about ten years. Wonderful experience—I got to do a lot of traveling, got to see a lot of things, as things developed I was there firsthand to see it. At the time Joe Louis had the fight with Max Schmelling and knocked him out that night in New York City 'round about '37—I was there that night. And it was so fast I didn't even get to see the fight. When I looked up it was all over with. And I couldn't believe what I was seeing.

Travel is one of the greatest educations a man ever had. With the limited schooling that I had a chance to get, and to have accomplished what I have accomplished, it had to be through will and dedication, believing in yourself, first of all. If you don't believe in yourself, nobody else believes in you.

As porters we had a lot of prejudice. But, you can handle prejudice, too, if you know how to handle it. We were together [in the union] and we tried to do the best for the masses—the most of us. We had some, of course, contrary like we have in everything; everybody's not going to see the same. But out of it all, we viewed our very wonderful way of life. We still stayed honest, we still believed that there was a better day ahead. And in order to be prepared for that better day, it's in yourself. I'll tell the world, if you want to get somewhere, believe in yourself. And if you believe strong enough in yourself, other people will believe in you.

As I was coming into my twenty-first year, nineteen hundred and thirteen, and of people who weren't born that I'm talking to today—in 1913, I was made a Mason. The Masonic Lodge is a name taken from biblical history—it comes out of a trade [stone masons]. People believe so in it that it comes to be part of their complete life—because if you were a good Mason, you were a good everything. If I live to see next March, I will have been a member of that order seventy five years—consecutive years—this is something that has never happened before, white or black.

When I went east, I took a trade—in the vending machine business. At that time the vending machine business was in its infancy. Nobody believed in machines selling merchandise. So we had a time to sell the idea. But we sold it to the extent that it's one of the biggest industries in America. And I was one of the pioneers who helped to make it possible. I was a master mechanic in the vending machine field—trained in building them from start to finish. I began the trade in Haverhill, Massachusetts in 1929. I went through the factory-school, and come out tops.

I took my trade in Massachusetts. And I stayed there for three, four years. Then I moved into New York, and had an office in the Empire State Building, on the thirty-seventh floor. So I stayed there until I moved to Hartford. The vending machine business kept me away from home all the time. I got tired of just living on the road. I was on the road constantly. I was married by then. And I got tired of that, and I said I'm going to settle down someplace where I can be of service to the community and myself. I worked for a company when I first came to Hartford called the Self Sales Company. And I worked for them for several years. Because I was only here five years when I went into business for myself. I went into business in 1945. I got the idea that if I can make other people's equipment work I can make it work for me. So I decided I would go into business, so I opened a vending machine business—vending, records and novelties. And I must tell you I was very, very successful. Some people say you can't make it because of who you are—because you're Black—but that doesn't always work. I knew sales, I knew what the people wanted, and I knew what I had to do to get it to them, and that's just what I did. And I was very, very successful. People didn't ask what color my skin was when they wanted a certain record or they wanted a certain piece of equipment of some kind, they wanted to know where can I get it? Well, if you

Some people say you can't make it because of who you are—because you're Black—but that doesn't always work. I knew sales, I knew what the people wanted, and I knew what I had to do to get it to them, and that's just what I did. And I was very, very successful.

go to Johnson's he can get it—if he can't get it, you might as well forget about it! That's the kind of reputation I built.

The same year I went into business, I joined the Elks Lodge—the new Nutmeg Lodge of Elks—in Hartford. I worked diligently with them. We bought the building, paid for it, bought another one and paid for it. And during that period I was elected as the Exalted Ruler—the top man. I served in that office seventeen consecutive years. By having performed such service, they made me "Past Grand Exalted Ruler of the Improved Benevolent Protective Order of Elks of the World." Meanwhile the Masonic Order [in which Johnson had maintained membership] bestowed on me the title of "Past Grand Master" of Masons in Connecticut by having served well in the community.

[Johnson retired in 1956; in 1966 he was asked to donate his services to Project Headstart—a government sponsored effort to improve early childhood education in the inner city.]

I happened to know one or two people—teachers—and they knew I wasn't on a regular job, and they got in touch with me and asked would I come and help them out. It wasn't so much for the money, it was something I wanted to do. I took care of all the equipment—the bicycles, toys, tables—if something needed repair, I was the man you'd see. I was in the vending machine business so anything mechanical, I could do something with it. Then later on, I took a job of taking the handicapped to certain schools. I joined a bus company that was doing that—worked for them for six years. I didn't think I'd be there six days. But the more I did it, the more I became attached—it's the way you treat kids sometimes—you can make lasting friends. If a kid loves you, he'll let the world know he loves you. And I had some of those kids get on my heart so I couldn't put them down. If I'd get sick, they wouldn't get on the bus, because I wasn't there to drive it.

[Later Johnson came to champion the cause of older persons.]

I went into the senior citizens group up at Tuscan Homes. There was man there from the Capitol Region Conference of Churches. They were talking about getting up a group to work helping to get certain laws passed for senior citizens for certain things that they were trying to do. One of the main things they were trying to do was to get the medicine bill—ConnPACE—passed [a bill to offset the cost of prescription medicine for older adults and the disabled]. Too much credit cannot be given to that organization called USA—[United Seniors in Action]. It was through them—and through the ideas that they were able to sell to all of the senior groups scattered throughout the city of Hartford—the same idea that we're going to do this thing, but in order to do it, we got to do it together. I heard him talking about that, and I said, "Gee, I'd like to belong to that. The Director said, "Come to the next meeting." So I came to the next meeting and found out what it was all about. And I was so glad I did, because it was down my alley—it was something that I wanted to see done.

When I first came to Hartford, you had one skyscraper here and that was Traveler's Insurance downtown. And since I came to Hartford, it's a new Hartford. I said to them down in Capitol Hill [where he lobbied for passage of ConnPACE], "Look out the window, just look all around you. Who do you think built those buildings? Those buildings were built by sweat, blood and tears from senior citizens. We're the people who paid the taxes, we're the people who made the decisions, and we're the people who saw to it that they were put into effect. Now, have we got to beg to get a prescription at a price that we can afford to pay, when we made Hartford what it is, when we made Connecticut what it is?" [ConnPACE was approved by the State Legislature, and is now administered by the Department of Social Services]. Was it worth the effort? Together you can win. Because we got everybody to see the same thing at the same time, and to do the same thing, and consequently we succeeded.

PART III

WOMEN LIVES: HOLDING UP MORE THAN HALF THE CONNECTICUT SKY

INTRODUCTION

Women's Lives: Holding Up More Than Half the Connecticut Sky

Ruth Barnes Moynihan

Women have always participated in the making of Connecticut history. Their work in both agriculture and industry, and in the cultural development of Connecticut society, has been just as essential as care of their families and service to others.

As English settlers moved into Connecticut during the seventeenth century, they found Native American women who were skilled in growing corn, gathering abundant oysters, clams and lobsters, weaving beautiful storage baskets, and even reconstructing wigwams each time the tribe moved from summer to winter or hunting and fishing camps. Indian women taught the uprooted European women about native medicinal plants as well as New World foods like corn, squash, beans and pumpkins.

In fact, women's household work during the seventeenth and eighteenth century encompassed many of the necessities which are now supplied by machines and supermarkets. Mothers and daughters, as soon as they reached age five or six, were responsible for large vegetable gardens; the preservation of a winter food supply; raising hens, pigs and cows; making butter and cheese; spinning or weaving thread, cloth; making clothing and bedcovers for their families; carrying heavy pails of water from a well or spring; cooking in forty-pound iron pots over hot fireplaces; nursing their own sick and helping out other members of the community in childbirth or in need; bartering with neighbors to exchange their own work for any goods they could not produce; and often running a tavern for wayfarers or a shop for the townspeople. Some women found time to embellish their work with artistic achievement in embroidery or quilting. Skilled midwives were recognized and employed in widespread territories.

Many women helped others with such endless responsibilities by working as indentured servants or slaves. Servants, often poor immigrants from England and Ireland during the colonial era, might work off the cost of the ship passage and eventually achieve freedom in their own households. Some Indian and most African women were enslaved for life; the total prohibition of slavery in Connecticut did not occur until 1848.

Communities of colonial settlers were usually gathered around the Founding Fathers of the local church. But Puritan Mothers were also avid Bible-readers, if they were among the fortunate ones who had learned to read, and their opinions about faith and spirituality became major factors in the great eighteenth century religious revival known as the Great Awakening. Both the mother and the wife of New England's greatest theologian, Jonathan Edwards, who praised their influence upon him, were Connecticut women of extraordinary character and intelligence. As towns grew and religious teaching diversified, it was often women who insisted upon the founding of new parishes closer to their outlying farm villages and the employment of more responsive or progressive ministers. By the nineteenth and then twentieth century the sustaining organizational and fund-raising work of women became indispensable to all the Protestant, Catholic and Jewish groups in the state.

The Revolution and its aftermath brought other changes in women's roles. While men were away fighting women had to take over family responsibilities, even though they did not yet have the legal means to carry out business—as the letters from Lois Peters to her husband, Captain Nathan Peters, demonstrate. Some followed their men to war, serving as the only cooks and washerwomen for the hard-pressed army. Many women, like Deborah Champion and Sybil Ludington, were spies or revolutionary messengers; they could slip through enemy lines or carry messages long distances on horseback without incurring suspicion from gentlemen Redcoats. Women also took on rudimentary political roles as they boycotted British tea and proudly wore homespun clothing instead of fancy British textiles. They organized to raise both funds and supplies for the soldiers.

After the war, the government urged women to increase production of silk thread (grown on their own mulberry trees in eastern Connecticut) or straw hats (in Guilford, Hartford, and elsewhere) or even onions (in the Wethersfield valley of the Connecticut River) to be exported to England and Europe, thus improving both the Connecticut economy and the nations's self-efficiency. Profits from onion-growing even enabled Wethersfield women to build their own church, becoming an often-cited example of female entrepreneurial skill for worthwhile causes. During the nineteenth century, having learned what they could do for themselves and their communities, women also sought more education and other social reforms. Academies were opened to provide women with some of the opportunities previously allowed only to men, and some women even began to train as teachers. Connecticut women educators like Emma Willard, Catherine Beecher and Prudence Crandall became famous throughout the country. Many others went west to teach in frontier communities, or south to teach the newly freed slaves after the Civil War.

Women also began to write hugely successful poems, novels, and essays. Catherine Beecher's *Treatise on Domestic Economy,* a how-to-do-it book for the "professional" housewife, first published in 1839, became one of America's all-time best-sellers. So did her sister Harriet Beecher Stowe's 1852 novel *Uncle Tom's Cabin*, a passionate portrayal of the evils of slavery, which made her world-famous. Writing was one of the few professions open to Connecticut women in the nineteenth century, and many made the most of it. Other women went as missionaries to the Far East, and a few women joined their sea-captain husbands on whaling ships, chronicling voyages around South America to Thailand and Shanghai and the Sandwich Islands at a time when most women could travel only in imagination.

Connecticut women were among the first to become active in the movement to abolish slavery in America. They formed anti-slavery associations all over the state, inviting famous speakers like Angelina Grimke and Abby Kelley for lecture tours, and gathering thousands of signatures on anti-slavery petitions to send to Congress. Many a courageous housewife risked arrest and imprisonment for herself and her family on the illegal "Underground Railroad," giving food, shelter and hope to escaping slaves as they passed from one hiding place to another on their way to safety in Canada. When the Civil War broke out, Connecticut women were among the many nurses battling the filth, misery and horror of army hospital camps, while other women worked diligently to provide the food, bandages and other supplies so desperately needed.

Throughout the nineteenth century, increasing commercial and industrial activity caused great changes in women's roles. There was more wealth and leisure for some, but definitions of "ladylike" behavior imposed greater restrictions on female activity. Outdoor exercise and physical labor were forbidden to "the better sort," and ladies wore tight corsets which distorted their bodies and contributed to ill-health. Increased emphasis on the responsibilities of motherhood, including the education of children (which had previously been man's work), also contributed to a gradual fall in the birthrate. Women wanted more time for each child, while theorists claimed that good women were naturally "passionless" and had a moral duty to spiritualize the "natural" brutality of men and the world. Unfortunately, this notion also led to an increase in prostitution; even in small towns, everyone knew which house the "bad women" lived in, while any woman who "lost her virtue" faced the censure of both family and community.

Meanwhile, factories had begun to employ poor women and children, as well as men, throughout the state. For many families, including the increasing numbers of immigrants who poured in from Europe in the later part of the century, a wife's wages made the difference between her family's destitution and survival, while young women could achieve a brief self-sufficiency—though most of them gave their earnings to their parents. Connecticut industrial development was greater than in much of the rest of the country, its watches, clocks, textiles and machine parts produced by a labor force one-quarter of which was female.

By the turn of the twentieth century other types of job opportunities also became available to some women. As department stores and office work expanded, women were hired as clerks, typists and secretaries. A few educated women became lawyers and doctors, though opposition remained great, while writers and educators continued well-established traditions.

However, the twentieth century brought both educated women and working women to a fuller awareness of their potential and their need for political, social and economic equality.

Suffragists campaigned for voting rights which were finally achieved by federal Constitutional Amendment in 1920. Women of all sorts worked for child labor laws, health services, legal and civil rights for married women, working women, and members of ethnic minorities. They participated actively in politics from 1920 on, many as members of the Legislature and town government bodies, as civil servants, and federal office holders, as labor organizers and leaders and, finally, in the person of Ella Grasso, as the first elected woman governor in America. An Equal Rights Amendment became part of the state Constitution in 1974.

Today the range of activities and accomplishments of Connecticut women is far too great to chronicle here. The following pages provide only a selected portrait of the lives and accomplishments of Connecticut women, some well-known, others anonymous. Their work, though still sometimes appreciated or unrecognized, continues to be essential and indispensable to the life of the Nutmeg State.

I

Hannah Heaton

Hannah Heaton (1721-1794) was born and raised in Southampton, Long Island (part of the New Haven Colony in her day). When she married Theophilus Heaton, Jr. (1719-1791), of the city of New Haven, she joined him and lived the rest of her life in North Haven. She kept a diary in which she recorded events and personal reflections from the time of the Great Awakening (a religious revival movement in mid-18th century New England) to the first few years following the American Revolution. The diary is largely a record of her religious development; the following excerpts recount spiritual "exercises" she underwent, often while carrying on her daily chores. It also reveals the ways in which her diary-keeping and spirituality helped her deal with what was apparently a very difficult marriage, within the bounds of 18th century notions of "wifely obedience." Her original diary is held in the collection of the New Haven Historical Society. [NOTE: Hannah Heaton used no punctuation or capitalization in her writings. These have been added and spellings "modernized" for readability.]

Diary, (undated). I went over to New Haven in the fall, just before that great work of God began, which was in the year 1741. There I heard Mr. Tennant and Mr. Whitefield preach, which awakened me much. I began to think my nature must be changed, but how to attain it? I knew not when I was coming from meeting to my quarters, which was about 6 miles; my company began to worry me to sing. I put them off 'til I feared they would be offended. At last I sung some verse about a contented mind. I thought that was better than to sing a song, but others little thought how I felt. It was hard work for me to sing.

I am now 50 years old and o' how much of this precious time I have lost. Almost 20 years I lived in a state of nature and I have lost all the other 30 when I haven't lived to God.

Diary, (undated). This week I ran away from my family and spent half a day in prayer. One night I went to bed sad and heavy. I dreamed that a Christian woman was with me, one that goes to our prayer meetings, and she said to me, "Bind the tears in bundles and burn them now." As soon as she had said that I thought I heard the great God speak. Thus let them alone for in a little while I will send my angel that shall gather the wheat into my garner and the chaff shall be burnt with unquenchable fire (Luke 3-17). Good part of the night I watched for fear I should forget this lovely dream. In the morning how refreshed I felt while I was making my bed.

November 1767. Ah poor me; with an anxious mind I sat away to go to New Haven. The tide being very high, the crossway was all over covered for about half a mile. When my horse had carried me about half way it stumbled and fell off the crossway in to the mire, and so I waded out about up to my knees. I ringed my clothes, rode a mile, got to a fire and got dry things. Lord I thank thee for preserving me from such an awful death and preserving me from taking cold. O' God let me always be in an act of readiness for death. O' let me never again be anxious about anything beneath the clouds. O' break down the power of sin in me, for his sake whose holy humanity was arraigned to die as a criminal hurried away to execution and hammered to the gibbet.

February 1 - 1768. This day I saw a man extremely angry for a mere trifle. I went away into the cow house with a soul full of sorrow. There I poured out my heart to God for him with a great freedom. I thought I was willing to die if I stood in the way of his conversion, or if it might be a means of it. Strong and powerful scripture arguments come to mind as I plead for myself and my family.

October 7 - 1769. One morning early as I was going to milking with a soul full of sorrow that word come to me with some sweetness, these light afflictions which are but for a moment shall work for us a far more exceeding and eternal wait of glory. But now scriptures seem only to help me while they are passing through my mind. Lord I thank thee for here a little and there a little.

October 26, 1769. I met with much sorrow from one that should be my best friend. O' the sin which I continually hear, great sins indulged, great duties neglected. It makes my heart ache and my joints weak. In the evening I went out a few rods from the house and tried to pray, but how shut up I felt. At nine I will try again. I know not that I can speak one word but I was scarse on my knees but I see my own and my family's case and spread it all before my God. My very soul cried. I wrestled hard in prayer to God: O' Lord have mercy or we perish. Now when I come in my husband was very angry because I stayed so long and he laid cruel things to my charge, and said he believed of a man in this place that caught his wife away alone with another man. Now my husband spoke such dreadful words I don't love to write them, and that night I might not sleep with him. The next morning he began to rage at me again. Then I up and told him that I was praying for him and for all. As I spoke a shower of prayer come upon me. I fell to praying loud before him with a flood of tears for some time, and that spirit in him was stilled. He said nothing but looked smiling and pleasant, and never said anymore about this matter.

November in 1769. The day after Thanksgiving I went without my dinner. I took my Bible, went into the barn and kept the afternoon in fasting and prayer (the weather was cold). I thought I felt my own and see my family's wants. I had liberty in prayer.

March 17 - 1771. I am now 50 years old and o' how much of this precious time I have lost. Almost 20 years I lived in a state of nature and I have lost all the other 30 when I haven't lived to God. I have been shut up this cold winter and endured much hardship. I have been to prayer meeting I think but twice since winter on the sabbath. O' how often am I drove to God in straits and have got help when I could hardly expect it. Ah, I am one that must be bound to heaven. Lord pity me. I fear when I write that I shall exceed on the right hand or on the left, I dare not put pen to paper without prayer. Now I was helped with a free mind to give something to a poor person for clothing to help them to go to meeting. Lord bless them in soul and body.

North Haven Historical Society

The Montowese Baptist church in North Haven. It was formed in 1811, in the building above on Quinnipiac Avenue, some 17 years after Hannah Heaton's death. Before that time, the Baptists worshipped in their own, or fellow Baptists' homes. The church was named for Montowese, the sachem of the Quinnipiacs in 1638 when the tribe sold land to the English which became the New Haven Colony.

[March?] 1772. Last week I was helped with a free mind to give a little money to a poor sickly family. Lord pity them for Jesus sake. Now I just received a letter from Long Island. Lord I thank thee for the sweet truths in this letter. Bless my friends and relations there with the choicest of heavens. Blessings o' God, and bless again that Isle in the sea. Now I write a letter to my two brothers and two sisters at Newark in the Jerseys. I was enabled to address myself to each one's particular case that their souls were in as I thought. Lord bless this letter, to their souls I beg for Jesus sake.

1772 July 5. Now we have the newspapers that tell of terrible things in righteousness that God is doing [throughout] the world. Now every man's sword seems against his fellow. There seem to be universal divisions, in churches and in families, oppression by cruel laws, pestilence and famine whereby millions have died and we hear of earthquakes in diverse places. O' methinks I see the scriptures fulfilling the end, a hastening.

October 4 - 1772. Mr. Beech preached from Psalms 84-11. He marked out the path of holiness and showed what it was to walk upright. It seemed good and teaching.

October 7 - 1772. The authority in this place went and took away three cattle from three of our separate brethren to pay their rates to Mr. Trumble [taxes were assessed by the local church]. Now when they drove Mr. Beech's cow away his little girl of [?] years old ran crying after them, begging for the cow. She told them they had stole the cow. They said to her they wanted to pay Mr. Trumble. She told them her dad did not owe Mr. Trumble anything, but they would not hear the cries of mothers nor children. The babe's father told me the child never heard anybody say a word about their stealing the cow but had a mind to go after them of her own accord. Mr. Beech's wife talked to the men, told them how wrong they did and they must be accountable to God for it. One of the men cried like a child.

February 18 1781. Now Jonathan and two of my neighbors had a bad contention arose between them. Now this man and his wife and myself are in covenant with each other, and now I heard of threatening words by this man of going to the law to have the case decided, and there appeared anger...for there are such things in our church already enough to make one's heart ache. I kept pleading with God for several days for help and strength that I might go as Abigail did to David. At last I went but o' what a sweet spirit I see in this man and his wife. They both said they was willing to leave it to men, and so I come home in peace. .

October 1781. Last sabbath Mr. Beech preached from Psalms 58: 3-4-5 verses. The word was good to me. Methought I fed upon it but o' now upon hearing that [General Cornwallis] and his army is taken. O' what shooting, frolicking and heathenish rejoicing is there is our town instead of giving glory to God for this smiling providence. O' God do pour down thy spirit. O give us true repentence. Pray don't let us provoke thee to give us up yet into our enemies' hands.

November 10 - 1781. I have a sense of expected trouble where there is so much sin. As I went to fetch a pail of water this word come to my mind. Let us endure hardness as good soldiers. Now I thought that a good soldier will not turn his back for fear of a few bullets, but will press forward, hoping to gain the victory. O' my God, give me perseverance.

November 13 - 1781. This day was a thanksgiving for the mercies of the years and for [Cornwallis] and his army, taken by our men this morning. This word was with some power on my mind. Humble yourselves therefore under the mighty hand of God that he may exalt you in due time. Lord humble me, I hope yet in thy mercy.

1782 [no date]. This summer past there has been an extreme drought. For many months the heavens were like brass and earth like iron wells and brooks dried up, flocks and herds ready to starve for grass, our latter harvest almost cut off. And o' at this time the righteous sad, the wicked mad whilst thou withholdest thy spirit. O' thou Jehovah, pray reveal thy arm, pour down thy spirit and we shall be turned.

January 7 - 1783. This day my Jonathan had another son, born about noon, and it died about sundown, a large lovely babe. Now glory to God for sparing the mother when in such immanent danger for many hours. Lord heal her, restore her to health if it be for thy honor and glory.

July 2 - 1787. I looked out at the door and see a company of chickens scratching and picking in the mud. How they prattled. It took my mind to see how content they was with what God had provided for them. I see that all God's creatures answer the end of their creation better than poor sinful man, unthankful for the mercies we have, and yet discontent because we haven't greater mercies.

[August?] 1787. I am still sorely afflicted with a distressing pain in my back. The Lord doesn't wrong me but he helps me yet to think and speak well of his name, although he is shaking me over the grave. But O, what a wicked worldly heart have I. God is daily showing me the vanity and emptiness of all things here below, and yet mere trifles will decompose my mind. I think that it is thirty or more years that we have kept bees and this spring we lost them all, but O how anxious I felt, though I begged hard submission and after a while I got still about it, and I think in June my husband took a swarm upon shares, and upon the 5th of August my little grandchild of almost two years old went out to the bees and a great great many stung him. The child cried as hard as he could about an hour and a half with the pain, and then went into convolution fits. His father went near four miles for a doctor and we feared every moment would be its last, but the doctor come and the Lord blessed the means so that the child grew better, and the next day run about the house. This was an undeserved mercy, but o' how I did beg for the child's life if it was God's will, for it was I that had sinned.

1790 [no date]. Now above a year I have had sore eyes and in April there was in the night a thunder-storm. There was one very hard clap. I thought the lightning seemed to hurt my left eye and I soon found it was blind. I was much distressed in my mind with fear that I could read no more. I got up, went to the fire, lit a candle, took a book. I found I could see to read with my right eye. Blessed be the Lord for his mercy who might justly have took away the sight of both eyes because I have improved them no more to his honour.

October 1790. My son Jonathan had another daughter born. The midwife was with her not much more than an hour before it was born, a perfect and living child. O' the mercy of God, when we were fearing she would be as bad as she used to be. Surely the Lord is a God hearing prayer. Before my husband died for half a year or more I heard it in my mind, the sound of death a'coming. It seemed very near. I often told my husband of it. I also told my daughter of it. I thought because I was so unwell it looked likely I must die first, but after he died my distress was took off my mind. The Lord is still gracious to me since my husband's death. I am well provided for. My children are kind to me. Their kindness sometimes melts me into tears—to think that the Lord should be so kind to me and move them to love and pity me, so vile a sinner. Lord I thank thee. Pray, Father, reward them with an interest in Thy love.

II

Lois Peters

Women in the preindustrial era participated in all aspects of the family economy, helping husbands to manage farms and trades and businesses as well as tending to other domestic responsibilities. But the legal system gave them no autonomy; a married woman could sign no papers, collect no debts, sell no property without her husband's signature. This became a particular burden in times of trouble like wars. Even with her husband risking his life as a Minuteman during the Revolutionary War, Lois Peters had to write to beg him for money because the law gave her no legal right to collect his business debts or carry on his saddle-making business independently. Nevertheless, she continued to manage their farm, as did thousands of other colonial women. The following are selected letters exchanged by Lois Peters and her husband Nathan. [NOTE: Spelling has been "modernized" and punctuation added for readability.]

To Captain Nathan Peters, Roxbury
Preston, June ye 20th at Night 1775

Dear husband,

I this Moment Take Pen in Hand To Let you know that I am well and all our Friends here. Have No News To write. We have heard of the battle [of Bunker Hill, June 17, 1775] you have had Among you but we hear So Many Stories, we know not what To Believe. A report This Morning was very Current here that General Putnam was Missing, but we had it contradicted before night and Said he was only Slightly wounded in the wrist. Our fears are Many but we all hope for the best. My Heart aches for you and all our friends there, but I Keep up as good Spirits as possible. If you Could Spare your Mare, I Should be very Glad if you would send her home As Soon as possible, for I Can't borrow at all and Should be glad you would Send me Some Money if you Can, but Don't let that Trouble you, for I am not Like To Suffer for any article To Support My Family but Cannot Carry on The Trade without money. But that is the Least of my Troubles at Present. Our Corn Looks well and our Work goes on as well as I Could wish. Pray write Every opportunity. It being Late, I Must Conclude with wishing you the best of heaven's blessing and hope that God in due Time will return you To your family in Safety. I am your Loving wife 'Til Death

Lois Peters

Should be very glad of four or five Pounds of money for without Some Money we Cannot carry on The Trade any Longer, for we have Laid out all the money we had for Leather, and 'Tis all worked up. I am not Like to want for anything To Support my family, father being free To help me To what I want for that but Don't Love To go to him for money To Carry on our Trade.

To Lois Peters at Preston in Connecticut, per favor Dr. Downer
Camp in Roxbury June 26th 1775.

Dear Wife,

I Received Yours by Doctor Downer in Which You inform me that You Are All in good health. I Could Not have heard more Joyful News. I am Well through the Goodness of God Who has preserved me to this Time. I have No News more than Doctor Downer Can Inform You. Our Enemies Fired on Us in this Camp Last Saturday and Again Last Night and Killed Two men. Pray Write Every Opportunity for it is A Great Comfort to See Your Letters. Am in the Utmost haste. Remember me to All Friends.

I am Your faithful Husband,

Nathan Peters

P.S. Send me Some Stockings as Soon as possible.

To Captain Nathan Peters at Roxbury
Preston July ye 2d 1750

Dear husband,

With great Pleasure and Satisfaction I Set myself Down To write a Line To Let you know that we are all well, as I hope these Lines will find you. I have No news worth writing at Present. Should be very glad of four or five Pounds of money for without Some Money we Cannot carry on The Trade any Longer, for we have Laid out all the money we had for Leather, and 'Tis all worked up. I am not Like to want for anything To Support my family, father being free To help me To what I want for that but Don't Love To go to him for money To Carry on our Trade. Mr. Button Says If we are willing he will go To Work for himself and board with me, and Says he will Take what Stock on hand we have for what we owe him and will Take it at what it cost and for his board will Let Saddles go where we owe, Particularly To Mr. Brewstar; he has had a Saddle for himself and wants another for his wife. I Shall Try To find Something for him To do 'Til I hear from you. Pray write as soon as Possible and Let me know your Mind about it. I Cannot Collect one copper. There is an account against Ebnz. Punderson, which is for Serving a writ on Amos Geer for 10 pounds. I want To know whether it is Said, for they almost Deny it and if it is due To you now Pray Send home a

Power of attorney To Dr. Downer and we can collect it. He is gone To York and it is Expected his family will go after him Soon and I think Such Men ought To Pay all Their Just Debts and Then be hanged. I shall send you Some Stockings the next opportunity. Am your affectionate wife 'Til Death,

Lois Peters

To Lois Peters at Preston in Connecticut, per favor Cpt. Morgan
Camp in Roxbury, July 9th, 1775

My Dear Wife,

In my Last Letter I informed you that I was very sick. I have Now the pleasure to inform you that I am through Divine Goodness in health as I hope You and All friends are. I Wrote in my Last letter to have You send me Some things Which I hope You Will Do As Soon as You Can, and I Would have You Send Joseph's Green Coat and UnderJacket. You wrote in your Last letter for Some Money; Capt. James Morgan, Who Brings this Informs me that My Money for Coming Down in the Alarm [Nathan Peters was a Minute Man, and marched in the Lexington Alarm of April 19, 1775] will be paid in one Week from this Time, Which Will Be About Five Pounds. I have Agreed With him to pay it To You and I Shall have Some here to Send to You in About Ten Days, I believe, So that You Will have enough to Carry on the Trade, Which I think Will be best. I Read Your Letters With Great Satisfaction. Pray Write often.

I am Your Loving & Affectionate Husband,

Nathan Peters

To Captain Nathan Peters at Roxbury, per favor Mr. Capron
Preston, July ye 24th, 1775

Dear husband,

I have but a Moment of Time To write. Capt. Stanton is waiting For the Letter but would Just Let you know that we are all well. I have Not received a Letter So Long from you that I am Tired of waiting for you to write. I hope you haven't forgotten your family. I have been very Much put To it To get help To Cut our hay. I am Like To have it all Cut Today. The Drought has been very Severe here and grass Is very Poor. We had a Small Shower of rain Last Night here which has Made a great alteration in the Look of the Earth, for it was as Dry before as Most Ever I Saw it. Pray write Every opportunity for it is all the comfort I have To read your Letters and hear of your welfare. You Talked of Sending Me Some Money to buy Something for me—maybe a gown, but I haven't received any yet for that Nor nothing else. It would be very kindly accepted Now, for I have found Just what I want but cannot get it without the Money. I talk of Coming Down To father's If opportunity of Company Should Suit and the weather Seem Pleasant. Should be glad of your advice about it but cannot write any More.

I am your Lovin' wife,

Lois Peters

To Captain Nathan Peters in the Camp at Roxbury per favor Mr. Freeman

Preston, October ye 12th, 1775

Dear Husband,

I take this Moment of Time To Let you know that we are well Through the goodness of God as I hope you are. Have No news More than Mr. Freeman Can tell you; father Sold our oxen before I got home To John Morgan for Ten Pounds. I have got my Corn harvested and have about Eighty Bushels. I hear you are going To Stay all winter. I am very sorry To Hear Such News but hope it is Not So, for I think you Can't Stay Consistent with any reason at all. It gives Me Great uneasiness To hear that you Talk Of Staying, but beg you will Not for I Can't think of Living alone this winter; am in great haste.

I am your Loving and affectionate wife until Death,

Lois Peters

[P.S.] If you Could Send me a Little Money by Mr. Freeman you do me a great favor.

III

Hannah Hicock Smith

Hannah Hicock Smith is chiefly remembered today as the mother of the five Smith sisters from Glastonbury, two of whom became famous in 1874 for their challenge to taxation of women without voting representation. Abby and Julia refused to pay their property taxes and the town of Glastonbury confiscated their cows and then some of their land, and the story circulated nationwide.

However, Hannah Smith herself was active throughout her life, especially in regard to anti-slavery causes. She organized the first petition campaign to Congress for the abolition of slavery in the 1830s. Along with her daughters she went from door to door, collecting signatures, as did many other women throughout the country, though the cause was then very unpopular. Having learned Latin, French, and Italian as a child, she taught her daughters to pursue knowledge and independent lives, while they all maintained one of the largest farms in 19th century Glastonbury.

Born in 1767, Hannah Hicock started keeping her diary at the age of fifteen, three years before she married the Reverend Zephaniah Hollister Smith. He was dismissed from his Congregational Church ministry because of his freethinking Sandemanian sentiments in 1790 (Mrs. Smith's diary describes their various moves for several years after that without mentioning the cause). He eventually became a lawyer and later represented Glastonbury in the state Legislature.

Hannah Smith loved reading and poetry, and her daughters later published some of her poems in a small book which is now in the Connecticut Historical Society collections. It was probably her love of poetry as well as of Latin which led her to choose her daughters' exotic names: Hansy Zephina, Cerinthia Sucretia, Laurilla Alleroila, Julia Evelina, and Abby Hadassah.

Hannah Hicock Smith was a widow by the time the following entries from her journal were written. She kept writing daily in her diary until April 1850, and died at the age of 83 in December of that year. Except for some of her early letters, only the diaries from 1840 on survive. The following are excerpts of entries from Part IV, July 15 to August 7, 1844, and from Part X, December 19, 1847 to December 25, 1848 [the original diary may be found in the Archives of the Connecticut State Library. The following, is a slightly edited version of excerpts].

July 15, 1844.

Six p.m. I hope now it will not rain but it is cloudy all our hay is cut and half of it out and has been these 3 days—Abby has made me two pens and I have better paper. I ought to write well and not write so many wrong letters. I could write a much finer hand, but I cannot read it so well. I have been helping Henry lay Stone round the well, and cannot see much. It certainly affects my sight to work hard, or steady, read or write long at a time, & certainly there is no need of it, especially in a journal, where I can write nothing amusing or interesting and very little worth setting down.

This is my birthday 77: I was born the morning of August 7, 1767. My eye is much better. I am in good health as we are all and we have met with no misfortune the year past worth mentioning.

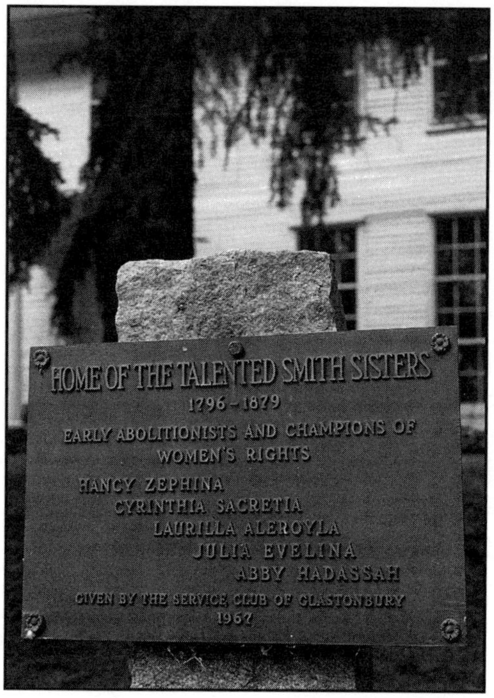

Tom Beardsley

Zephaniah and Hannah Smith's home still stands in Glastonbury. A plaque in front of the house recalls the exotic names of the couple's gifted daughters.

July 16.

Today it began to rain about one o'clock in the night tho' I slept so well that I did not hear it till about four when I rose, it has rained very steadily all day till now it slacks, but does not clear off. I have been mending all day an old loose gown that is not worth it. So I spend my time when I do anything. Yesterday sold Esq. Brower 5 bushels of corn at 64 cents. It is rather cool, I should say it is a North East storm. It does not smoke in our back kitchen when the wind is east, and we can have a log on as we have today to iron by. Yesterday Z[ephina] carried Mrs. Peltan ten pounds of flour which she is to replace but, I guess never will—I was almost sorry I cut this paper in this manner, but, I believe it is, on the whole, more handy.

July 17.

7 pm. Slept tolerably rose with the sun clear & bright, has been so all day which has done us a great deal of good. Our hay is all in the barn without any damage worth mentioning. In the forenoon we took all the corn from the hogsheads, 24 bushels, put it in barrels after pouring it out in the sun; most of the chaff went off. I have not done much beside work in the corn house & pick red raspberries have eat some in milk, perhaps too many, I shall see.

Almost ten. I am rather sleepy but will write this line Z has been to see Mrs. Weaver. Carried her some crackers. She gave us some dry'd beef and is recover'd. She had dropsy.

July 19.

Today I have contrived to do enough outdoors to tire me. It is a little cooler at least there is much wind. Cynthia & Julia are gone to Hartford. It is very still here today, no teams or noise. They were to come home by this time, to go a hurtleberrying this afternoon. It's growing warmer and is gathering some clouds perhaps for rain. Oh it rains some. There is a cloud spread all over. No thunder till just now. It looks as if it would not rain much, I pick chips, carry in wood, fix the fence &c.

July 20.

Today it has rain'd very much almost all day, it is clear now. I have work'd in the garret putting up things, almost all the forenoon & cleaning bee boxes, which is more than one would think, as I have cleaned only two or three—read in old translations this afternoon & I read every day in old journals 60 years ago & 61, how time gets along, the days go off very fast to what they did then.

July 22, 1844.

Monday p.m. 3. Rose with the sun. Today we kill'd a calf. Mrs. Porter dressed the head and feet on shares, or she had half, & half the inwards Z & C have been up street to distribute half a quarter. We have wash'd today. Mr. Porter brought in our rye from the wheat pen. I have been gathering it in the barn. I cleared the barn floor before it was brought in, with Henry. It has been good weather, but it is warm, and somewhat cloudy now; my pen is getting poor. I will mend one, I do not think this is as good, but this does a little better.

July 24, 1844.

Today, Wednesday, I have been tolerably well; have done very little beside fix the pendulum to the clock; have slept some. It is very warn & clear this afternoon. Z has carried out wool to the carders but I thought I should card a little today but I sweat enough now.

Yesterday a young Dr. Erving, his wife, and sister Charlotte who wrote for Freedom's gift drank tea here, took a book of my writing, was to bring it back today—will let me see hers.

July 25.

Today Henry and I have taken up with matches a beehive hardly any bees, full of millers. It took me till 8 o'-clock to clean it and melt the bees wax. I have helped fix the cheese press. Julia has made a cheese. It is cloudy weather has sprinkled some and Dr. Erving and sister came this forenoon, brought my book and a paper of her brothers, who is a poet. She is to send me the evangelist, which I believe has some of her poetry in it. It has been quite a rainy day tho it does not rain now. It looks as if it would be a rainy night. Maynard's grain is out and not stack'd, looks like rain.

but if it clears off tomorrow it will not be damag'd I think; Dr. Erving took some currants for his mother who lives in Hartford. Although I do not write very well, I have a good pen, I mended it. Tomorrow our papers come but they are not worth much, they are so full of politics. They do not tell much news.

July 26.

Today I did chores, boil'd bees wax, mended the kitchen table till ten. Z went to see the calves. Julia and Abba are gone to the Post Office. Z has been to Mr. R's to get the brass kettle mended, has got is done and brought home. It seem'd this forenoon as if we should have fair weather but it has clouded up. Looks some like rain again. It has been very poor hay weather for sometime tho' our hay has been in the barn a week, at the same time it had one share of rain on it.

July 29.

Today Henry and I went to whitewashing fences. I whitewash'd the back side of the back kitchen, did not sleep, am tired. Betsey is here. Abby wash'd. Z does the wash. Julia has been to Mrs. Weavers. Z and Hen has been to see the calves and one is lost, she is going tomorrow morning after it. Last even went to bed half after nine rather tired.

July 30.

Today Z. and H. went early and found the calf with the others. We have three 2 heifers and a steer. Henry and Wallace are getting in our grain. It is very fine weather. Mrs. Weaver is here, Z went for her in the morning. Betsey is gone to Dea Hale's to assist. He has inflammatory rheumatism.

Seven - Zephina is gone home with Mrs. Weaver. We have all our grain brought in, it is fair but looks some like gathering for a storm in the west. Went to bed half after 9.

July 31.

Today it began to rain about six and rains as steadily as tho' it would rain all day. Hen and I have put up a little wood but I do not do enough to set down anything. Read the old journals. It is sixty one years ago, today, since Pata Sheels and I went to Milford to her uncle's where we had a droll visit, went to New

Haven next morning accompanied by the eldest son who was more civilized and then rode home in very good spirits, and in good season.

Seven. It has rain'd all day. Rains now, notwithstanding which I have been at work setting a post and clearing rubbish by the maple tree with Henry, got wet and have made a fire in the stove. Betsey is here. I have carded some today.

August 2nd, 1844.

Friday a.m. I rose before five. Last evening went to bed half after ten. Today it is very warm indeed. I have been nailing on boards to the fence near the wellsweep and fixing whitewash for the front fence. Henry is doing it, and am rather tired already, but I must do something or I am not contented. Julia makes cheese.

August 7th.

Today I wak'd at four, but do not rise till I hear breakfast setting. Our girls rise at five. I have been to the cowyard to feed chickens. This is my birthday 77: I was born the morning of August 7, 1767. My eye is much better. I am in good health as we are all and we have met with no misfortune the year past worth mentioning. Have had a sufficiency of everything, my health has been good except a few weeks of nervousness, Laurilla four or five weeks of influenza and Abby about as long sickness with bilious fever. I received a letter from Francis Hicock [her brother] some days ago, which I shall not answer till I have been to Southbury. I think I shall go next week, with Laurilla and Henry, he is going to Hartford today after shingles.

Half after ten. I have been at work in the garden and have stepped into Dea[con] Hale's to fix the pointer of his clock, it had fallen down. It grows very warm, clear and pleasant otherwise.

Two p.m. I have slept. Betsey is here, Abby is at Dea Hales. I have really nothing to do, or nothing I want to do any more than I had the day I was sixteen. I was then full of inconsistencies but do not write them so plain now. I wanted to see Grey and but the evening before I thought Grey unworthy of pursuit, as I expressed it, I was then somewhat nervous, as it appears, had a pain in my neck and fear'd anything evil—My eye is almost well. I make no resolutions now as I did sixty one years ago, I could not keep them then, one was not to write so bad any more. I am sure I could not keep it now tho' I cannot see to make a pen and a steel one is hard to write with. I must tell Francis that we must correct ourselves and not ban everything to old age.

December 19, 1847.

Sunday 4 p.m. clear, warmer, poor going. Rose past six. L. made the fire, read in the papers, the answer to the Message from the Intelligence. It is capital. Julia gets supper and Z breakfast. I have caught water from eves. They have run briskly. It is for washing tomorrow altho' the hogshead is full. Sixty-one years ago yesterday, I moved to Newtown in a Sleigh. My mother and Mary Johnson was with us, our house was new and unfinished. Two stacks of chimneys and a space quite thro' the middle which with a north large bedroom were filled up commodiously and front room, kitchen & two small bedrooms were plastered. We lived there near four years, and moved to Southbury, which then was Woodbury. The beginning of April 1790 where we lived till February 7, 1792, then moved to Glastonbury. Eastbury, lived there, where Julia was born, till May 1st 1794 when we moved to Windham, lived there one summer till October then moved to Glastonbury North part, opposite Philip Sellew Esq. one year, and in October 1795 moved to the middle part where we have lived ever since. How soon the time is going and we are gone, nearly all my former acquaintances are dead. I know of but 5 or 6 living of my age in Southbury.

December 20, 1847.

Monday 4 p.m. cold, cloudy, freezing. Rose early made the fire. Z got breakfast, L, Z and I wash'd, L, Z and I went in the farm wagon to Mill & to the Tinner Treats. Got 4 cents old pipe, miserable going. They bro't the meal and bran of three bushels rye and carried some corn. I cut a pot of apples for tarts. It was a serious job to cut rotten apples. I pick'd them out last Night, I have been taking extracts from Cultivator. L. is one to exchange them at Mrs. Child's who owns them — I have been reading my Father's Journal and I find in December the 15th, 1769 he began a school in Southbury. The School-house stood opposite Dea Hicock's, 2 miles from our house. He kept school several winters, and was so importun'd by the inhabitants of Southbury to keep a high school, that in the year 1774, we removed there, in the spring. I lived there nine months in the house of Eleazer Knowles about a mile above Dea Hicocks. I was seven years old, and remember driving the ducks with Pata Sheels, and my mother learn'd me to spin wood that Summer. My uncle Francis Hinman lived in our house and when we moved back we lived with him, his family a wife and 3 daughters, about my age, till the spring, or beginning of Summer, when his new house was ready for him.

December 22.

Tuesday 5 p.m. quite cold, clear. Rose early, Z made the fire, she gets breakfast early, by candlelight. The ground is frozen hard, and it is so hubby in the road that a wagon going sounds like a drum. It must take some time to level it. I was thinking how we used to get along when I was young, and there were no wagons at all, but we used always to ride horseback and I suppose had a foot path, the road was trod otherwise only by oxen and carts, In those days it was the fashion to ride double, or two on a horse, and a man would carry his wife to meeting on behind, and a child before. However, I had a horse to myself as also my cousin Belharia and sidesaddles of our own. Many a mile have we rode so, for exercise and diversion, being rather proud of having each a horse signal, as it was uncommon—I am writing alone in the dining room, Laurilla has a stove in her north bed chamber and Julia in the south, C[erinthia] and Z[ephina] in the North front chamber and Abby in the south, so we keep 5 fires and 5 candles or lamps—I have been making tart-pies today, and have done better than I tho't I could.

December 23.

Thursday even 6 cold weather and clear. Rose at 5 made the fire felt very well as I have all day; done nothing but pitch in wood and mend a pair of stockings and help nail on boards and fix the bee house, in doing which my fingers almost froze as well as Laurilla's. I read my journal 64 years ago. It was the most interesting time of my life, I was sixteen, and the more I was noticed, the less I would see company except occasionally when I was with my cousins Johnsons, and as it were accidentally. There were then four daughters of them, 3 older and one a little younger than I and they had a great deal of company, some of them were with us part of the time and I was there as much. All are dead but one, and all the ladies and young men educated at

Yale College. Nearly all of which die in a very few years; I have been spared more than twenty years longer than any of them, except one. She dies last year, but only spared, perhaps, to see that all is vanity and vexation. It is melancholy to think we live so little time, and yet to so little purpose. It seems as if time flew faster every year, every week and even every day, till I think of what my mother said, that the days were nothing and the time seemed like nothing, but getting up and going to bed.

December 24.

Friday evening 8 somewhat sleepy cold, not extreme, clear. Rose before L about half after 5 made the fire. Zephina engag'd to go to Hartford and she went, with A, and L, though as it snow'd last night some and exceeding bad travelling, they got two muffs and everything else they chose, I suppose about 15 dollars cotton cloth, callico, oil, sweet potatoes, and wrought nails. When I was young we had no other, but in the revolutionary war we tho't every old nail was of consequence, and every old piece of iron, as indeed, we did every other thing, for there was none to be bought, I have seen children's frocks pinned with thorns, I have seen wooden tea cups and saucers in some families, but we could spin and weave our garments. Happy were the daughters whose mothers had laid by a gown or two of silk and callico or chintz. My mother had a comfortable number altered for me when I was in my fifteenth year. The war did not end till I was near 16, when we began to buy, tho' cloth of all kinds was dear—the clock strikes nine, I must go to bed—I wonder why I am tired, when I do so little, cut and bake applies, fetch in wood. Saturday 2 p.m. dull times, Dull weather Christmas cold, cloudy. Rose late, had rheumatism, C made the fire, bowl of bread and mild for supper. Slept from 2 to four. Russel moved the sleigh, and the girls rode down in it, to get the horse shod, he slipt considerable going down and it is miserable sleighing.

Tom Beardsley

The Smith family graves can be viewed in the graveyard, adjacent to the buildings of the Glastonbury Historical Society.

IV

Isabella Beecher Hooker

Isabella Beecher Hooker (1822-1907), younger half-sister of Catherine Beecher and Harriet Beecher Stowe, organized Connecticut's first Women's Rights Convention in 1869. The previous year she wrote a tract entitled "A Mother's Letter to a Daughter on Woman Suffrage." It was originally published anonymously in Putnam's Magazine November and December, 1868, and reprinted under her name as a tract of the Connecticut Woman Suffrage Association, of which she became president. We present it here not only for its historical value, but for at least one heart-felt response that has been preserved, and which follows Ms. Hooker's letter.

MY DEAR DAUGHTER:

You ask me what I think of the modesty and sense of a woman who can insist, in these days, that she is not sufficiently cared for in public and in private, and who wishes to add the duties of a politician to those of a mother and housekeeper. Let me begin by asking you the meaning of the word politician. Having consulted your dictionary, you reply, "One who is versed in the science of government and the art of governing." Very well. Now who is thus versed in the science and art of governing, so far as the family is concerned, more than the mother of it? In this country, certainly, the manners, the habits, the laws of a household, are determined in great part by the mother; so much so, that when we see lying and disobedient children, or coarse, untidy and ill-mannered ones, we instinctively make our comments on the mother of that brood, and declare her more or less incompetent to her place.

I am charged with the crime of desiring to meddle with politics, and to educate my daughters as well as my sons to take an intelligent, and, if need be, an active part in the government of their country.

Now let me suppose her to be one of the competent ones who, like your Aunt E., has helped six stout boys and four of their quick-witted sisters all the way from babyhood up to manhood and womanhood, with a wisdom and gentleness and patience that have been the wonder of all beholders—and let us think of her as sitting down now in her halfforsaken nest, calm, thoughtful and matured, but fresh in her feeling as ever she was, and what wonder if she finds it hard to realize that she is unfitted either by nature or education for the work of law making, on a broader and larger scale than she has ever yet tried.

Her youngest boy, the privileged, saucy one of the crowd, has just attained his majority, we will say, and declaims in her hearing on the incompetence of women to vote—the superiority of the masculine element in politics, and the danger to society if women are not carefully guarded from contact with its rougher elements—and I seem to see her quiet smile and slightly curling lip, while in memory she runs back to the years when said stripling gathered all he knew of laws, country, home, heaven, and earth, at her knee—and as for soiling contacts, oh! my son, who taught you to avoid these, and first put it into your curly little head, that evil communications corrupt good manners, and that a man cannot touch pitch, except he be defiled."

I have taken the bull by the horns, you perceive in thus taking our mother from her quiet country home and setting her by imagination among the legislators of the land; but it is just as well, because the practical end of suffrage is, not eligibility to office merely, but a larger use of this privilege than most women have ever yet dreamed of, much less desired.

And now she is there, we will say, in the legislature of our State—a high-minded, well-bred woman; one who, amid all her cares, has never failed to read the newspapers more or less, and to keep alive her interest in the prosperity of her country, whatever the claims of her numerous family. She is one, too, who has not had the assistance of wealth in doing all this; she is, as you know, straight from the rural districts, a genuine farmer's wife. But she has more leisure now than she once had, and with it there comes a longing for change, for more cultivated society, for recreations and diversions such as her busy hours have seldom afforded her; and just now, by the unanimous vote of her townspeople, she is sent to our glorious old Hub, to spend the winter in considering what the Commonwealth of Massachusetts shall do this year, by legislation, for the public good. Having secured a home not far from the old State House, she seeks the Assembly Room and meets there gentlemen from all parts of the State—farmers, merchants, and mechanics, physicians, teachers and ministers, lawyers and bankers, and they go into debate on such questions as these: Shall our deaf mutes be educated at home, or in the Institution at Hartford, as heretofore? State Prison—shall the discipline be penal merely, or reformatory? The institution self-supporting by a system of rigid tasks, or partially supported by the State? What punishment should be allowed, what religious and moral instruction furnished and what sanitary regulations enforced? The prohibitory law—has it proved itself adapted to the suppression of intemperance? Are its provisions enforced, and why not? The school for juvenile offenders—is that managed judiciously? Here obviously the great aim should be reformation. Is a system of rewards or punishments, or both together, best adapted to that end? Should boys and girls be associated in the same buildings and classes, and for what length of time should they be retained for improvement before sending them out again into society? Endowments for colleges and other educational institutions, supported in whole or in part by the State: Shall these be confined to institutions designed exclusively for men, or shall they be applied equally to the education of both sexes? Prostitution—shall it be licensed as in the old countries, or left to itself, or subjected to severe penalties? Divorces—by whom granted, and for what cause, and upon what conditions? Common schools, and high schools, and the whole system of State education; insane asylums, poor-houses, jails, and many other institutions of modern civilization: in all these objects, you will perceive, our mother has a deep and intelligent interest, and it is not difficult to imagine the warm, even enthusiastic energy with which she will give herself to the discussion of the questions involved—some of them the highest that can come before a body of legislators.

If you say, There are other State interests with which she is less familiar, I reply, No one legislator is prepared by his previous habits of business and thought, to deal intelligently with all the questions that may come before the House, or is expected to; committees are appointed for specialties, as you know, and composed, or they ought to be, of those whose education and training have fitted them for that special investigation.

And so in all matters pertaining to merchandise and business, which fairly come under state jurisdiction; it is late in the day to assert that women know nothing of these things, and could not learn if they should try. There are too many honest and successful women—traders, artists, and literateurs in every city of the land, and too many men dependent in whole or in part upon their earnings, to give a show of color to such assertions.

On the whole, then, my dear, you begin to perceive that my mind receives no shock when I am charged with the crime of desiring to meddle with politics, and to educate my daughters as well as my sons to take an intelligent, and, if need be, an active part in the government of their country; and I am convinced that these sons will not fail ere long to be the first to recognize the propriety and wisdom of such a course on my part. The truth is, that one chief reason why young men oppose the extension of suffrage is, that their sense of true gallantry, their desire to shield and protect, is violated by their conception of the probable result of a woman's going to the polls. This is certainly a misconception. Every woman knows in her own heart that she does not hold her purity and delicacy subject to injury by such cause. We know that we have never entered any precinct, however vile and debased, without carrying something of that god-given power of womanhood—of motherhood—with us, which is a greater protection against insult and contamination than all the shields that man can devise. But we ought not to blame men too severely for their reluctance to relinquish this office of protector and guardian, which custom has so long laid upon them as a high duty and privilege.

In the days when physical forces ruled the world, men might naturally offer, and women receive with thankfulness, the protection of a strong arm, and become greatly dependent upon it, without serious harm to either sex; but in the day of moral forces it is quite otherwise. This day has come upon us, however, so silently, so gradually, that we ourselves have scarcely recognized that we are now near its noon-tide: how then can our fathers, brothers, and husbands, be expected to feel its quickening glow and inspiration?

I am persuaded, contrary to the judgement of many earnest advocates of equal suffrage, that women are quite as much responsible for the present condition of affairs as men, and that they, as a body, will be the last to be convinced of their duty in the matter of good citizenship; so I am seriously anxious to make converts to my faith from the young mothers, rather than from any other class. I know, of course, that the power of regulating suffrage now lies wholly with men; that not a single vote can be given, save by them, and I am convinced that the indifference, not to say opposition, of their wives, mothers, and sisters, stands in the way of their coming to a right solution of the problem before them,, beyond anything and all things else.

I am always your affectionate____

Isabella Beecher Hooker's letter reached many Connecticut women, among them a Norfolk farmer's wife, who wrote the following reply (no response from Hooker has yet been located). [The original letter is now part of the collection of the Stowe-Day Foundation in Hartford, CT.]

October 24, 1871.

Mrs. Hooker or Madam

Excuse the boldness of this communication, as I write to you as a friend, for you are a friend to us all. And without further preliminaries, let me state my case.

I am a farmer's wife—in this little hill-side town, having been here seventeen years. I have no children and have only the dreary routine of household cares to occupy my mind. My husband is an old-fashioned farmer, and plods contentedly on year after year without a mower or reaper, without books or anything to make home pleasant. His amusement is to go to the village store to spend his evenings and rainy days, while I amuse myself by mending his old pants, or some other equally agreeable occupation. I have often asked him to allow me to take some child to care for, but this he will not do. It involves expense. Of course, such a man is bitterly opposed to "woman's rights" and loses no opportunity for the usual sneer. I have no money and but few clothes. He forbids my giving anything away, as everything is his and nothing mine. In short, I'm nothing but a housekeeper without wages, doing all the work of the family. I have no fondness for this kind of life, but on the contrary have as keen a relish for amusements, concerts, lectures, etc., as any woman in the city of Hartford.

Now, Mrs. Hooker, please give me a little advice. Is it my duty to spend all my life in this way? Would it be wrong for me to go to Hartford this winter for a few weeks or to some other place where people live? Have you any friend who would give me a pleasant home, and an opportunity to attend an occasional entertainment in exchange for my services? If you ask what I can do, I reply I can do what women in the country usually do. I can sew, or do anything that is necessary to be done—can take care of children and teach them, as this was formerly my employment. I must get away from here for a while or go crazy. Perhaps you will say I am already deranged.

My husband's father buried his fourth wife a few days since. She laid down the burden of life willingly, at sixty-two years of age. He will doubtless marry again soon, as it costs too much to hire a housekeeper. You are my first and only confidant in this matter. If it seems worthy of a reply, please address:

Mrs. S. H. Graves.

P.S. I have omitted to say that this husband of mine has bonds, stocks, and notes and to these he is wedded.

S. H. G.

The Stowe-Day Foundation

Isabella Beecher Hooker is pictured c.1902. Hartford's Stowe-Day Library has a Hooker collection of more than 1,000 items, dating between 1834 and 1907. From 1869 onwards, Hooker corresponded regularly with suffrage leaders such as Susan B. Anthony and Elizabeth Cady Stanton.

The Stowe-Day Library is located on Nook farm, the 19th century Hartford neighborhood in which Isabella Beecher Hooker, Harriet Beecher Stowe, Mark Twain, Charles Dudley Warner, Joseph R. Hawley and William Gillette lived. The library focuses on the architecture, history, literature, decorative arts and woman suffrage movement of 19th century America.

V

The Conditions of Wage-Earning Women and Girls (1914)

For many middle class women in the late nineteenth century, and into the twentieth, having a wage-earning job was a liberating experience, providing income and independence. But for many working class women and girls, it was necessary to go to work in order to supplement family income or often provide the sole means of support. The following are short excerpts of interviews conducted with anonymous workers in a variety of settings in Hartford, New Haven, Bridgeport, Waterbury, and several other cities throughout the state in the early part of the twentieth century. They talk about wages, work conditions and their families, and make poignant comments about themselves and others. [These selections are from a report published in 1914 by the Bureau of Labor for the State of Connecticut on "The Conditions of Wage-Earning Women and Girls."]

• I am eighteen. I am a Russian Jew, and have been working for seven years. For three I have worked here and for the rest at home. I can make pants as good as any man. I made them when I was twelve. I get six dollars and I give it all to my father. My father does not work any more. We have five working in our family, there are eleven children besides. My father gives me two dollars a week to buy me clothes and everything. I can't do it. Some day when I can save I am going to run away to New York. A girl, to be decent, ought to have eight dollars a week.

A girl, to be decent, ought to have eight dollars a week

• I was fifteen last December. My father is dead. I get two dollars fifty cents which I give to my mother. She makes Aunt Kate's dresses over for me. I wish I had some money to spend, ten cents of my own to go to the movies. We met a man once who was going to take five of us. My mother wouldn't let me go. I don't have no good times. We can't get no money because they ain't making no money.

• I am thirty-four years old and receive $18 a week in the cloak department. It takes ten dollars to pay my board and car fare and I find I can't save hardly anything on the rest. I have to dress well. I get clothing at a discount from the store. I have an endowment insurance and will take another one as it is the only way I can save. I think women need more money to live on than a man. I am sorry for the kids that have to work, they ought to be home. I do my own laundry and make all my clothing except suits.

When I get through nights I go to bed. I am too tired to go out. I am a bundle girl and stand all day. You ought to see my ankles swell. I get three dollars fifty cents. No, I didn't ask for more, for it wouldn't be any use. I wish you would ask them not to take orders so late because it keeps us awful busy, and folks could buy something in the mornings if they had a mind to.

I don't think it is fair to say that girls in stores are worse than girls out of them. I can show you girls in New Haven High who walk down Chapel Street and get 'pickups,' and then tell their mothers they were introduced. I think the girls in stores are wonders to be as good as they are and stand what they stand from some snippy things that are no good. I don't see any harm in having a gentleman friend to take me to the show and give me a feed afterwards. It saves the price of a meal ticket. Us cheap paid girls gets it, but just look after some of the old hens that are in with the bosses and queening it around.

• I am seventeen, I have been working nine months, my mother is dead; we have seven in our family. I'm oldest, I get up at five and fix my father's lunch box for him and get the breakfast for everybody. I wash the clothes nights and iron and cook and mend. I wish I got more than five dollars a week. Father has only had three days at the Underwood typewriter factory, in Hartford for ever so long. I get kind of tired standing, but s'posing they sent me home? I'm lucky to have work.

• I am forty-six years old and have been here for twenty-five years. I kept right on when I got married, for I wouldn't put any man against $18 a week. He's dead. The firm is all right. The ones that get poor pay ought to hustle and get more. I believe it is all right for the firm to get the most they can for their money. Poor wages for others don't bother me.

I get twelve dollars a week in the suit department. I have worked here for eight years. My husband is dead and I have three small children. I have a flat with two rooms that about pay the rent and I have my home besides. I am going to educate my children. I think there is too much difference between the wages paid to the young girls beginning and the older help. I would like to see the girls get a dollar a day. It would help keep them straight.

Both my mother and father died on the way to America. I was here first, my aunt brought me from Russia. We are five. I get five dollars a week, pay a dollar for my brother Samuel to my aunt in New York. I pay $2. 50 a week for my board and a dollar for the board of Morin, Neva, and Rachel, to my aunt here. I have fifty cents to buy clothes for us. My uncle is a peddler. I made this from a grown-up dress. I fitted it myself. I cut it out by newspaper to look like me. At night I help my aunt to wash clothes and cook. We have nine in her family and six boarders. The children make flowers and take out bastings in the night.

• I get twelve dollars. I am head of the notion department. I have found girls getting so little that they used to steal. I have a son eight years old and pay board for him and me six dollars fifty cents a week and our laundry is a dollar. I go around evenings selling corsets and make enough to save a little to educate. It means working day and night.

I don't think much of this interview thing, anyway, and I hope they stop it next year. I don't think it is any of your business what I get or how I live. If I was the merchants, I'd stop the whole thing quicker than a wink.

I get a book of car tickets and ride in from Glastonbury to Hartford. I bring my lunch. Saturday night it is awful going out. I am afraid of my life every time I get off the car until I strike the house. But I have to do it as long as they keep open Saturday night. I blame the people for that. I guess if some of them knew the time the girls had getting home, they'd have a heart.

My mother goes out working every day and my sister and myself work in the store. As soon as we can get enough of money, we will have a little flat. We all live at the Sisters of the Holy Ghost. Lots more would live there if there was places. Lots of girls have gone to the Y. W. C. A. I know lots of girls who won't go to church Sunday mornings because they haven't clothes and they need sleep.

Yes, there are some seats in our store, but Mr. ——— will prance up and down before you like a mad man if he sees you sitting down twice in the morning. He does it on purpose to scare the girls so they are afraid to ask for a raise. I bet you won't find two in the whole store that have had their wages raised. I asked for a raise two years ago and I got such a talking to that my mother had to sit up with me all night. There is not another store in Bridgeport like this.

Tom Beardsley

Eastern Connecticut State University's Center for Connecticut Studies (left) has a number of excellent collections, including bound volumes and microfilm of Connecticut's Bureau of Labor Statistics Annual Reports. The preceding interviews were gleaned from the 1914 report.

Connecticut's Bureau of Labor was established in 1885 by the controlling Republican Party to attract Connecticut's rapidly growing urban working class vote. Connecticut Governor Henry Harrison appointed Yale's Arthur Hadley as Connecticut's first Labor Bureau Commissioner. The Knights of Labor dismissed him as a corporate stooge, but his 1885 Report roundly criticised corporate Connecticut, and the controversial Hadley was dismissed in 1887 by new Republican Governor Phineas Lounsbury. Nevertheless, the bureau's annual reports became established, providing historians and researchers a valuable window on Connecticut's labor history.

VI

Mrs. Donato

Immigrant women in this state often endured great hardships, not only in undergoing the journey from the old Country to the distant shores of Connecticut, but also in adjusting to new surroundings. However, the traditional cultural role of houseworker persisted. Mrs. Donato, an Italian immigrant [interviewed c. 1939 by Emil Napolitano for the Federal Writers Project (W.P.A.) Ethnic Survey] talks about the still unrecognized scope of that job, requiring a woman to be a Jill-of-all-trades.

And men want to know what women do all day

And men want to know what women do all day. Early in the morning I get up to prepare my husband's breakfast, then I get the children out of bed and get them ready to go to school. They have breakfast, too. Two of them go to school and the little ones keep me company. Then I throw two windows open to air the rooms, make the beds and start to get dinner ready. By this time it is almost twelve, when the kids be coming in, and my husband comes over every noon, so here it is dinner time and everything is got to be ready. Oh my, oh, my, how time flies, the morning goes so quick that I don't know where I am at, can you imagine that? And suppose you want to know what I do in the afternoon and the rest of the day. Well in the afternoon after the kids go to school, my husband goes back to shop, I wash my dishes and clean up a little. Then I do some sewing or washing, it all depends what day of the week it is. Sometimes I iron clothes. There is so much ironing to do that I get disgusted. The kids use so many dresses, that alone keeps me busy. Anyway it is already 3:30 and the kids be coming home. They want bread with butter or a piece of cake or some cookies. And the same things starts get supper ready.

Can you do that? I mean, fix the cord to the iron? I do, you bet. I'm the carpenter, I'm the electrician, I'm the painter, plumber, everything around here. I fix cords, change sockets, fix lamps, put in curtain rods. Sure I'm good. I'm the jack of all trades. I painted the kitchen set. I'm gonna sandpaper that old rocker, then revarnish it and put a nice finish on it. And I'm gonna put a new cover on the seat.

VII

Edna Purtell

The movement for universal suffrage reached a peak in the early 1900s. Through the efforts of tens of thousands of activists, pressure was mounted in every state in the union; in 1920 the Nineteenth Amendment to the Constitution was ratified. One of those who participated in this movement was Edna Purtell, born in Hartford in 1899. Her mother was a cigar stripper, her father a cigar wrapper. She was active in the tobacco strippers union in the early 1900s (in the 1930s she fought child labor in the tobacco fields); supported the independence of Ireland, and became the youngest woman to be arrested for picketing the White House during the suffrage movement in 1918. An advocate of women's rights throughout her life, she described herself as "an old-time militant suffragette." She was interviewed by historian Carole Nichols in her home in West Hartford on June 18 and July 8, 1980, as part of a Connecticut Humanities Council funded project, "The Political Activities of the First Generation of Fully Enfranchised Connecticut Women, 1920-1945." (The interview has been edited into a continuous narrative.)

I was born on at home, in Albany Avenue in Hartford, on February 9, 1899. And the snow was up to the horse's stomach! My father's name was Thomas Michael Purtell. He was born in Binghamton, New York, near the Pennsylvania border. He came to Connecticut because he was a cigar maker. He came here because, I think, they were on strike where he was. He came here to get a job.

I used to remember Katherine Hepburn outside the Strand Theater. She gave out [suffragette] posters.... and asked me to go to Washington to demonstrate. I said "Mrs. Hepburn, I haven't got any money to go to Washington." She said, "Will you go if I pay your way ?" So that's how I went. I was arrested four times in one day.

When he was only nine years old, he was apprenticed to the cigar industry. He was a member of Samuel Gomper's union, the first union in the country. They were independent, the most independent union. I remember when I was on Mather Street [in Hartford] that Samuel Gompers came to visit us. What they were fighting for in the cigar makers union was to have the black man included in their union. My father was so intelligent. He said, "They are using them against us." I always remember him looking up and saying, "Oh yes, I'm going to fight to see that the black man is admitted to our union, because they have to pay as much as we do, five cents for a loaf of bread." After that, that set me going to fight for what my father was fighting for.

My mother was born in Ireland in 1862. She came to Binghamton, New York, where she met my father, when she was only about fourteen or fifteen. She went to work. She went with the cigar industry, stripping tobacco. The women did the stripping. The men made the cigars, rolled the cigars. They were the most intelligent union. They had somebody read to them every day. Then they made up the cigars that the person who read to them would have made. They were aware of everything that was happening. Not only that, but I remember my father coming home and saying—he called my mother None—he'd say, "None, I've got a dollar assessment taken out because there's a strike up in Boston," or "there's a strike in New York." They supported the other strikers. My mother was also a union member. I also worked in the tobacco industry while going to night school to study English. I was secretary of the strippers union when I was sixteen years old.

My mother used to vote on the school question when I was a kiddie. She used to say—and I must have heard it and taken note of it—that they wouldn't appoint a Catholic girl as a teacher. Yes, they would discriminate against a Catholic girl. So, I remember my mother saying, "We can vote for the school committeemen. Why don't you go out and cast your vote? Why don't you go out and vote for someone who will allow it, won't be discriminating against the Catholics." So, I got interested in women's suffrage. [Edna knew that women were being arrested in Washington while demonstrating for suffrage.]

I used to remember Katherine [Houghton] Hepburn outside the Strand Theater [in downtown Hartford]. She gave out posters. I used to see them. I was in Brown Thompson's [a department store in Hartford] and Mrs. Hepburn came along. I used to help them give out posters. They used to call me "Little Purtell." She said, "Little Purtell, could you go to Washington?" and, you know, be arrested and demonstrate.

I said, "Mrs. Hepburn, I haven't got any money to go to Washington. I can't afford it." But I did have a week's vacation coming from the Travelers [Insurance Company, where she worked in the filing department]. I said, "I've got a week's vacation coming, but I can't afford to go." She said, "Will you go if I pay your way?" I said, "Certainly I will!" So, that's how I went. In August, 1918. I was arrested four times in one day, while demonstrating for the federal amendment for women's suffrage. I was so young. I could climb the statue, and a lot of women couldn't do that. I could climb the statue and call out, "Lafayette, we are here!" in Lafayette Park. I was arrested for climbing the statue.

They would take us down to the jail. Then they'd let us go. The older women, a lot of the women, couldn't go back, but I went back four times. I remember I carried the flag, the American flag. Then I carried another flag, and it said, " I come from Connecticut, the 'Cradle of Liberty'." The thing is that when we were arrested, it was the police who did it [soldiers were also brought in to arrest suffrage demonstrators]. We were very, very peaceful. All we did was carry the flag or say, "Mr. President, how long must women wait for liberty?" We were peaceful. It was the police who came in and arrested us.

We had banners: purple, green and white (Green and white and orange was the Irish). Purple, white and gold. I had that on. This was the last time we were arrested; in that day, four times. A young policeman came over. They got orders to take those banners away from us. So, I said to him, "Oh, I can't give you this banner. This banner is my banner of liberty. No, I can't give it to you." He said, "Well," and he turned away. A great big cop, a great big fellow, came along. He said, "Take it away." The young cop said to him, "You take it away." He proceeded to take it away. He bent back my fingers, and he broke two of them taking it away. Most of the women went on hunger strike for five days, but I went on a hunger strike for six days, because I wanted to go to mass before I went to court. I wanted to receive communion. When you go to mass and receive communion, you can't have any breakfast, anyway, but I hadn't, so I was six days on hunger strike.

Most of the women went on hunger strike for five days, but I went on a hunger strike for six days, because I wanted to go to mass before I went to court. I wanted to receive communion. When you go to mass and receive communion, you can't have any breakfast, anyway, but I hadn't, so I was six days on hunger strike.

My fellow workers at Travelers heard about this, and they put up a sign, "Votes for Women." When I came back, Batterson called me down. He was president, I think, of the Travelers at that time. He said, "You know, Miss Purtell, you're liked very well here, but we don't want you to be talking about suffrage and so forth." So I said to him, "Mr. Batterson, during work hours I'll take care of my job. But once I get in that elevator, what I talk about is my business, not yours. And on our coffee break, that's our coffee break, and I'll talk about anything I want." He looked at me. I found out afterward that his mother was interested in suffrage.

Hartford Studies Project, Trinity College/Hartford Public Library

American women won the right to vote in August, 1920, with the ratification of the 19th Ammendment to the US Constitution —so Edna Purtell's arrest just two years earlier was not in vain. Connecticut was a veritable hotbed of activity in the suffraget movement. To the left, members of the Connecticut Women Suffrage Association (CWSA) pose outside their Hartford HQ, c.1916. Below, the interior of the Association's offices and reading room. On the wall to the left are posters for the Prohibition and Socialist Parties, and a lar map of Connecticut. To the right, pamphle books and pennants are for sale to raise funds for the cause. By 1918, the CSWA had 77 statewide leagues, with 27,500 members.

Hartford Studies Project, Trinity College/Hartford Public Library

VIII

Helen Malloy

A latter-day champion of education and equal rights is Helen Malloy. Born in the Parkville neighborhood of Hartford on January 25, 1897, she taught for over fifty years in the public school system, before "retiring" to spend another several years as parochial school instructor. Co-founder of Hartford's first teacher's union, she was instrumental in improving conditions of work for teachers, as well as pay equity, including equal pay for women teachers (who constituted the overwhelming majority of teachers when she began her career). She was interviewed, at age 90, by David Shuldiner, on May 21, 1987, for the program "An Active Age," broadcast on Hartford Community Television.

[Parkville] was always part of Hartford, but it was really like a little rural village. The trolley cars came from downtown Hartford, stopped right at the edge of Parkville, and from there on you walked, unless you were fortunate enough to own a horse and buggy. So we were part of Hartford, but Parkville was just like a little country town, and Hartford was a small, but beautiful city. Now it's a big city, and Parkville is an active part of it. I lived there all my life. Taught school there all my life, except one year, when I graduated from high school, when I taught in a one-room schoolhouse in Bloomfield. I always did very well in school. I skipped two grades—the fourth and the seventh. So I got to high school at the age of twelve, and graduated at the age of sixteen. So it was through the encouragement of my mother—it was her ambition to have a teacher in the family—and the encouragement of my grammar school teachers that set me on the road to teaching.

My first class (in 1916) had 48 pupils—six rows with eight children in each row—that was in the fifth grade. But of course discipline was nothing in those days, compared to what it is now. Children were sent to school to learn, and they were sent to school to behave themselves.

As it so happened, my father had a very serious operation that summer that I graduated. One of my teachers, Miss Stevens, at New Park Avenue School encouraged me to go up to the Capitol [in Hartford] and take tests, which at that time, if you passed them, would enable you to go teach in a country school with what they called a statutory certificate. So of course we wanted to get some money in for the bills from the operation. So I went up and took the tests and passed them and I got a job in Bloomfield. It was a one-room schoolhouse. I had five grades and nine children. And the woodshed was at the back of this classroom. And my brother and one of his pals went up with me the Saturday before school started to get the wood all piled up in the woodshed so it would be convenient for me for kindlings and burning logs. We had this old-fashioned stove right in the middle of the room, in which we had to keep the fire going all day in the winter.

There was a trolley that left the center of Hartford—the Bloomfield trolley, and it went up Blue Hills Avenue, and then went over through the fields, and turned north into Bloomfield. And then I got off that trolley in the center and walked two miles to my schoolhouse. Up to that time I'd hardly been down to the center of Hartford. It was like another country to me. I was still only sixteen, so it was a big adventure.

In the summer, my father got me a position in the factory where he worked in Parkville—Whitney Chain—and I worked there for the summer to get some money, and then in September I went to New Britain Normal School—now Central Connecticut State University. It was a two-year teacher's college. I graduated in 1916. Right away, I got a position in what was then the south school district of Hartford. In the south and southwest area, there were six schools in the district. I taught at New Park Avenue—that was the school in Parkville. The building has been torn down, and they have what they call the Parkville Community School now.

I knew quite a few of the children, and my first class had 48 pupils—six rows with eight children in each row—that was in the fifth grade. But of course discipline was nothing in those days, compared to what it is now. Children were sent to school to learn, and they were sent to school to behave themselves, and in general, if the teacher had any complaints, all she had to do was write a note home, and that was the end of the problem. Of course, teaching in those days was very different than what is now. Movable desks were unheard of—everything was in a row. And the teacher's desk was right in the middle of the front—open space where she had a bird's eye view of everything and everybody. So it was really very different. I trained in all the grades. When I started teaching, I started in the fifth, and for a little while I was in the fourth, and then I went to the sixth, and I found my niche there. I never wanted to leave that grade. We taught ancient history, which was very interesting, and the children were still children, and yet they were big enough to do many things for themselves, so you could allow them quite a degree of freedom. But they hadn't reached that smart aleck stage that they got to in the seventh and eighth grade. So when I had a chance to go up into the seventh and eight I didn't take it—I wanted to stay in the sixth. Many times during the war years [World War II] when the boys came back from the front—I remember especially three or four boys of Italian ancestry that I had—they came to see me, and they said, "Oh, Miss Malloy, when you were teaching us about Rome, I never thought I'd see it. I couldn't believe it when I was there."

Helen Malloy saw many of her students go on to work and raise families; many of them left the state. She remained a resident of Hartford, and single—one reason being the prohibition against marriage for teachers. [Most were women in their early teaching years].

I remained in Parkville all of my life. Not that I didn't go places, and do things, but that was my home base. In fact I live on the same street where I have lived since I was about two or three years old.

As I grew in experience and learned what life was all about, I changed some viewpoints. I remember when schools were consolidated [in the early 1930s]. We had districts in Hartford when I started teaching, and then at one point the schools were consolidated. Some people thought that money could be saved by having the schools consolidated rather than in separate districts. That was quite a change—and that's when we started a unified teacher's organization. I was the secondary secretary of that—it was called the Teachers' League. The motivation was that now the school system in Hartford was run by one big organization, one school board had charge of all the schools. Before, when we had districts, we use to have district meetings, and we could go and speak at those district meetings about things that we thought should be done or could be done. Or we could talk them over with our principals, so that they would be brought up at the principals' meetings. But, of course, when the schools were consolidated, we teachers were more or less left out in left field. So that was the purpose in starting an organization, so that we would be able to meet with the school board and press our views.

Many times during the war years [World War II] when the boys came back from the front—I remember especially three or four boys of Italian ancestry that I had—they came to see me, and they said, "Oh, Miss Malloy, when you were teaching us about Rome, I never thought I'd see it. I couldn't believe it when I was there."

One of the key issues was the difference in men's and women's salaries—quite a difference. Another thing—and it took us many years to correct it—the salary schedules of all the various districts were different. So when the school board was initiated, they set up a uniform salary schedule, but they didn't put everybody on that schedule. They took you—wherever you were in your salary—and moved you into that schedule going up one step. So still, all the different people in the city were on different salaries. So getting the women on a scale equal to the men's and the elementary school teachers on to a scale equal to the high schools—those two things we accomplished first. And then getting the whole salary schedule straightened out—getting rid of what we called the inequities. I was secretary of the Teachers' League for a couple of years. I was president for about ten or eleven years. And then I left the League, and with the help of a teacher in the Northeast Junior high school, we formed a union—A.F.L-C.I.O [the first Hartford Teachers Union] about 1947. Ray Bialeck and I—he was in the north end of the city and I was in the original south district—decided to form the union. The pay inequities, that was still the big issue, and it was the union that finally got that straightened out.

Before I left the League, I was able to get, of course with the help of the other members, the Hartford Teachers tenure bill, the second one in the state. After three years probation period a teacher would be on tenure, and if she didn't qualify for tenure she had to be notified at the end of her three years. And there were only three conditions for firing a teacher—insubordination, incompetence, or immorality. And she had to have a written notice a certain time before the end of the year that she was being considered for dismissal—in writing, and stating the grounds and giving her a chance to appeal, and to appear before the board—if she wished with a lawyer—all these things were written into the tenure bill.

The tenure bill was almost accidental. They have a cut-off date for the Legislature, after which you can't enter any bills. I picked up the paper one night when I came home from a meeting, and I read that the cut-off date was two days away. So I called the man who was the legislative chairman of the League—a Mr. Smith, who taught in a high school—and he said, "Well, Helen, I can't get over there, but if you can get over there, see what you can do." I already had the New Haven bill, so I quickly drew up a bill based on the New Haven tenure bill—they had the first one in the state—and went over the next day to the Capitol with it, and one of the legislators introduced it for me. It took a long time to get it passed; we didn't get it passed until just before the end of the Assembly, and it went through after a lot of work.

Helen recalled the hair-raising experience she had getting a pay equity bill passed.

We were unable to get it through the city board of education, so we had tried to get it through the Legislature, and Joe O'Rourke, the secretary and business agent of the Connecticut state labor union—A.F.L.-C.I.O—he attempted to put it through the Legislature for us, and he got it through—it had already passed the Senate, and we got it into the house. But the Legislature was split that year. The Senate was Democratic and the House was still Republican. We had the bill on the desk in the House, and a recess was called for a conference on the budget. Our bill was resting on the desk, and while they were having the conference, our salary bill disappeared from the desk. So when the House reconvened and the bill which had already been called for was not found, Joe O'Rourke came running to me and asked me for another, and that was the only copy we had there. So they adjourned the House; they couldn't agree on the budget and they adjourned the House. Of course, that was the end of all our hard work. That was when we had the League, but after we formed the union, that was our first priority in the union, to straighten out the salary inequities, and we did accomplish it then.

IX

Rosa Montez

Rosa Montez (a pseudonym), a Black Puerto Rican woman, has experienced many obstacles, yet she has persevered to become an active community organizer in the neighborhoods of New Haven. She was interviewed by Rosemary Nardi on August, 1975, for the Ethnic Heritage Project, University of Connecticut. It has been edited into a continuous narrative.

I was born in Yabucoa—that's an Indian name. Yabucoa—Puerto Rico. That's in the southeast part of the island. And it's a very small town—it was. Now, it's a larger town. It is on the coast. We do a lot of fishing. I bring up the word fishing because it's a characteristic of the people on the coast that's different from the ones on the inside of the island. We do have a lot of Indian customs. We have different kinds of faces and our vocabulary is different in the coast than in the center. We just can't understand each other. It's sort of like two different cultures.

I think that if you are a woman and you're Puerto Rican you really have to work hard. And no matter how hard you work, still you won't make as much as a man. Because you are a woman, and we come from a patriarchal society.

Now we are changing. We used to fish and we have agriculture. We have sugar mills. We're one of the towns that has a sugar mill. So we weren't too poor, the town. We were sort of like in the middle. When I was thirteen days old my mother went to be a maid. She used to cook for a doctor, and she worked with this family until I was about twelve years old. And we have another lady, who's an old lady. She used to take care of us—my sister, my brother and myself. She didn't have any place to live, and she came with us so she stayed with us until she died. And she raised all of us—my sister and my brother too. My father died when I was four. He was a barber.

My mother was a good person. Made me what I am today. Because she—I can remember her—she was ironing after she comes home from the house where she worked as a maid all day, one to two o'clock in the morning, so that we'd have additional money. She took in other people's ironing and washing. Saturdays and Sundays she would do the same thing. She used to bake. She was a wonderful baker. She used to make doughnuts. We'd sell them in the schools. That's why I hate doughnuts—I used to get up in the morning, let's say, from the ages of eight until I was about fourteen years old, and I'd have to fry about five, six, seven hundred doughnuts every morning before I'd go to school. My mother would cut them and I would fry them. That was just to get additional money. My mother quit school when she was in sixth, seventh grade. Then later on in life she went back—by the time I was in high school she was also in high school at night. And she finished—we both graduated the same year in high school. And she continued her education. She became a teacher when she was 43 years old. And afterwards she was a social worker. She was also involved in politics. She was one of the founders of the Popular Party, which is still governing the island. And she was heavily involved with the community work. I was also. I was practically raised involved in politics—since the age of five years old.

School was sort of like an obsession with her. "I'm going to make it. I'm going to go back to school." That's one of the things she always emphasized with us. That we would have problems to overcome. We did have the problems with the races, the problems with the classes. And one of the things that she always used to tell me was "remember that you are Black. But you have to be proud of being what you are because I am Black and I'm proud and I'm going to make it." I heard that from my mother all the time.

I came here on April 6, 1948. My ambition at the time was to study law, and I was accepted at a university in Puerto Rico. But we used to have a physical before we go to the university and at the time I have a spot in my lung. Two days before I was supposed to start my college, I was called in and I had taken another X-ray and then they decided that I had to stay out a year, resting, because I had tuberculosis. I suffered a lot with the stigma of tuberculosis at that time, because it was a contagious disease. My cousin was here in the states, and I decided to come with her. And I've been here ever since. My sister was living in New York City. And I lived in New York City for almost 19 years. And then I moved to Connecticut.

It was hard to work in New York because I was under age, but I did work. I remember I used to make 16 dollars a week when I first started working in a factory putting on flowers and the feathers for the hats. My cousin was about 35. She was living with a Puerto Rican girl that married an American. My cousin is white. Her husband is white. And this family she was living with on 103rd Street was white. Automatically they thought I was white. But somehow color was never discussed. And when I came in and here I am dark, they told my cousin that—after a week—she'd have to move. Because they never realized that I was dark.

I got sick again, and I had to go to a sanitarium—to a city hospital on Staten Island. I stayed a whole year in the sanitarium. And after that I got married. And I kept going in and out of the hospital. I stayed in New York for all this time. Usually working in the garments. I used to work in girdles. I used to work all kinds of machines making girdles. And bras. I was really making good money. Then I separated from my husband. And I have a daughter and a son by him. And later I met my second husband.

I lived in New York almost 19 years, and I was tired of the same routine. One day I was going in the subway and I met one of my classmates from Puerto Rico. And he asked me, "What are you doing?" And I said, "Well, I'm working in a factory." He said, "What?" I said, "Yes, I'm working in a factory." He said, "You mean to tell me that you are a nobody?" He said, "Could you explain it to me? Of all our classmates I thought that the one that was going to make it was you." I said, "Well, I think I'm somebody." But those things stay within me. And I said to myself, wait a minute, what am I doing here. Am I really a nobody? Have I something that I could do? And I get to evaluating the things that I'm doing, and thinking about my mother and all that—by that time my mother was dead. She died in 1962 from an accident that she had while she went to investigate one of her clients. So I decided to start looking around and I sort of made up my mind that I was going to leave New York City.

A friend of mine was coming down from Hartford. And she asked me if I wanted to come along with her. And I did. And my husband came along with me and he liked it over here so he applied for a job at Pratt and Whitney, Hartford, and they accepted him. So in the meantime, I went to the Visiting Nurses Association in Hartford and I took an exam, and I scored about a year equivalent of college. And that sort of gave me some kind of motivation. And I came to live in Hartford. I didn't like it at all.

I didn't get to know anybody there. And we were living in West Hartford. And I didn't like it at all. My son was in Puerto Rico at the time. And my daughter was with me. My daughter was 11 and my son was 10.

Then I had a friend here in New Haven and I called her and I said, "I got to get out of here because I don't like it." And I said, "Can I go over to New Haven and like it better there?" She said, "Yes, come along." So I came down to New Haven and I like New Haven better. So my husband asked for a transfer from Hartford. And I started working at Berger Brothers. They made girdles and bras. In there I worked for about six months. And then from there I went to work at Strauss-Adler. They also make girdles. And I worked at Strauss-Adler for about a month.

In the meantime I went to a meeting down here on Legion Avenue about police-community relations. That was 1967. I met a person that is an alderman now. When I was at the meeting he pushed me aside and I was very vocal. And he said to me, "You know what, you're Spanish and you're so vocal, they're going to offer you a job in CPI (that was Community Progress, Incorporated) to shut you up." I just laughed. But then after that sure enough they did. And I started working for CPI in the summer of 1967. And I worked for them for a year. My position was homemaking advisor for CPI. While I was there I was involved with helping welfare recipients on budgeting, counseling and education. Taking them out to different health agencies. And it was very good, because there weren't many Puerto Ricans in community work. It was a good year because it gave me sort of like the foundations. It gave me a base to see how much help was needed in everything in the city.

I stayed a year at CPI. Then from there—that's when the Hill House Center was in the planning stages. The university [Yale] had submitted a grant to HEW [the federal Department of Health, Education and Welfare, now Health and Human Services] to start a health center in the hill community. They decided they needed to hire a black person—I mean Puerto Rican person—in the department of health, education, and community organization. So I was hired by the Health Center, Yale University, as health education assistant and community organizer. I stayed with the Hill House Center for three and a half years. I had the opportunity while working at the Center, to audit two courses at the Yale graduate school of Public Health .It was a good experience because I was never exposed to college life before. Then later on I decided to go to Albertus Magnus College. So I guess the Hill House, really what it did for me was open up some doors and give me some of the knowledge as far as the resources so that I could start going on. When I was working in the Center I was active on different boards—New Haven Mental [Health] Association, Yale Neighborhood Corporation, City Demonstration Board, Police-Community Relations Committee.

[Rosa joined a coalition of Spanish-speaking neighborhood organizations in the greater New Haven area. At one point it was called the Latin Council.] I was vice-president of the Latin Council. Then the Latin Council in the community had a meeting and they decided that they wanted to change the name and they wanted to change the structure. We came up with what is today the Junta for Progressive Action. It's a corporation. I was president of the Junta for two years. And then I went to work for the corporation as assistant director from May 'til September. We didn't have any more funds for the position of assistant director.

And I resigned and went to work for Home Agents Service Bureau. My responsibilities there were to supervise homemakers, and to work with different programs such as transportation. For two years I stayed in the homemakers service bureau and then from there, I'm in the last job that I have now, as director of the Puerto Rican Youth Services. This is a youth component of Junta for Progressive Action. We do have programs working with the juvenile court, the police department, the board of education, office of mental retardation. We have counselors for the parents. This past year for the board of education we have a part-time Puerto Rican psychologist. I used to come to the center and test the children and work with the parents. We have a good relationship with Yale University because—I guess I was fortunate that I was involved with Yale University for a while in my community organization activities. I was a member of the medical school committee, working on the recruitment of blacks and Spanish. And I worked hard so that more Puerto Ricans would come to Yale.

[on problems within the Puerto Rican community in Connecticut:] In New York, even if you were poor and you were white you would have to take the same kind of discrimination that we were all taking because we were living in the ghetto. But when I moved to Connecticut, that was shocking to me. Because I had some of the same discrimination from my Puerto Rican people here that I was having on the Island. In Connecticut most of the Puerto Rican people are from rural areas and the colored people that you have here are not as educated as the ones you have in New York. So it's a completely different kind of community. The people from the rural areas in Puerto Rico are nice people. But then you have the ones that come from the cities with the same kinds of values and classes and all kinds of hang-ups. And they're no different than when they were on the Island.

[on women within the Puerto Rican community] I think that if you are a woman and you're Puerto Rican you really have to work hard. And no matter how hard you work, still you won't make as much as a man. Because you are a woman, and we come from a patriarchal society. That is changing, but it is not changing as fast as we would like it to.

IX

Linda Buchanan

Although women have successfully taken on many occupations from which they have been long excluded, they are still often looked at as "oddities" and made to feel "out of place." Acceptance may come, but it's not an easy road. Linda Buchanan, a machinist at Pratt & Whitney, addresses this issue as she comments on women and work in the context of changing technology. She was interviewed by Robert Asher on June 1, 1981, for the Connecticut Workers and Technology Project.

Before I was a machinist, I worked as a retail clerk and as a waitress and various things like that. My job right before I decided I wanted something more of a trade, was as a retail salesclerk. It was a low paying job with virtually no benefits and long hours, and it was not a job that you wanted to be in and make a career out of for any length of time. So I decided I really wanted something else. At the time there was publicity about new opportunities for women in non-traditional fields and things like that. I had a friend who was going through a toolmaker's apprenticeship. She was making a lot more money than I was and had a lot more job benefits and protections, so that interested me.

You need a really thick skin and a real sense of humor to survive the initial months in a situation like that because you're like somebody in a zoo, you're like an animal in the zoo, that sort of thing. For a month I couldn't tighten a clamp without somebody coming over and making sure I had it tight enough. They didn't believe I could do it. I couldn't bend over the table to put a part on a fixture without the whole line turning around watching me bend over the table.

So I went around to different factories and tried to get a job where I could get some on-the-job training. I went through that process for several months and just couldn't get anything, because I had no previous experience whatsoever and I had no training, so they just repeatedly said, "No. We are not interested in talking with you." And I couldn't really find any training programs either. Finally, what I did, I ended up with a little assembly job at General Electric, a little old circuit breaker assembly line, which was more money, but it was a really back breaking, totally unskilled job, where I just put the same piece in a thousand circuit breakers an hour, over and over again. But I figured that would be a way to get started because a lot of other places said that you never had any experience in manufacturing at all.

And then, I got laid off from that. I had been hoping maybe they would have some training programs that I could get into once I was working in the plant, because that's the way I figured some places did it. If you were inside you had a lot better chances getting into an internal training program than if you were trying to get in from outside. I got laid off from there and while I was laid off, I went to Goodwin Tech in New Britain, which is a state vocational technical high school, and they have adult evening courses. So I took a night course in basic machining because the problem I always ran into was, "You don't have any training, you don't have any skills." And then I still had trouble. I couldn't get hired in East Hartford (Pratt & Whitney).

I applied at a lot of places. Finally I went to Southington Pratt & Whitney and just came on really strong and said I wanted to be a machinist and I had taken this night course; it was like twelve hours of basic machining, so at least I recognized what a lathe was and I recognized what a milling machine was. They sent me to interview for a job as a vertical turret lathe (vtl) operator. They said, "vtl op." I didn't even know what it was because they don't have those kinds of machines in little technical schools. And I called up one of my friends. "What's a vtl? Quick!" But I got the job and I worked as a vtl operator and after about six months there I transferred to the East Hartford plant, because I lived in Hartford and it was more convenient for me, and I worked as a vtl operator in East Hartford. So all of my training as a vtl operator, which was my initial training as a machinist, just came from learning on the job, from other operators.

I was the first woman to work in a department of about a hundred male vtl operators, so it was very interesting. I think it can be very difficult for a woman to go into that situation, and they had had some women first of all, just turn down the job, not even take it because of the atmosphere, the intimidation of the machine, and the fact there wasn't another woman in sight anywhere in the place. They had other women try it and just get discouraged. You need a really thick skin and a real sense of humor to survive the initial months in a situation like that because you're like somebody in a zoo, you're like an animal in the zoo, that sort of thing. For a month I couldn't tighten a clamp without somebody coming over and making sure I had it tight enough. They didn't believe I could do it. I couldn't bend over the table to put a part on a fixture without the whole line turning around watching me bend over the table.

So you encounter attitudes ranging from very helpful people—and without them you wouldn't make it—who will show you things and teach youths, who are very encouraging, to open hostility, to the constant, "What are you doing in this place? Why don't you go and get a nice clean office job?" And the answer to that is always, very simply, "money." I want to be making the same money. So anyway, I made it, and now they have a few more women but you still find very few women. There hasn't been any big breakthrough. You still find a real token number of women in jobs like that and it still can be a very difficult atmosphere.

XI

Eleanor Boyle

Since the 1700s, insurance has been a major industry and source of employment in the state of Connecticut. And like other industries it has seen a great deal of change, both in the character of work, and the character of the workforce. Eleanor Boyle (b. 1920), who worked for Travelers Insurance Co. from 1938-1986, has not only experienced these changes, but has also taken on the responsibility of challenging a traditional division of labor in the "white collar" world where, for a long time, women held little more than clerical jobs. She was able to break down this barrier, through perseverance—and a little help from her (women) coworkers. The following are excerpts of an interview conducted on April 20, 1989, by Tracey Wilson.

Tracey Wilson: Can you tell me about your first day at work?

Eleanor Boyle: Oh yes, very vividly. I went to The Travelers on November first, nineteen thirty eight. I was in the stenographic department. I had applied several times and finally was hired. I was attending Morse Business College at the time, and I left when I got the job. The first day they took me up to the chief supervisor's. There were several young women in her office. Apparently they had not been hiring because of the Depression. A clerk came and took the other women away, and left me. Well, I died a thousand deaths. I thought they were just going to say sorry, they couldn't use me. But finally another clerk came up and took me to the group department's stenographic pool. In the middle of the morning, one of the girls asked me if I would like to go to the ladies' room, and I was so afraid they'd think I was wasting time, I said, "No, I don't have to go." On my lunch hour, instead of going over to the cafeteria I ran up to Sage Allen's cafeteria, went to the ladies' room, had my lunch and ran back, so I'd be sure to find my way to the seventh floor in the tower building. I remember it very vividly. Today, you would be escorted to the company cafeteria on your first day.

When I told my boss I was going to retire, he said, "You're going to retire? I thought you were going to stay until you were seventy." I said, "Well, I've worked forty-seven and a half years, I'm in good health, and I think it's time I left and played a little."

TW: You were pretty nervous.

EB: Very nervous.

TW: Now, had you graduated from high school?

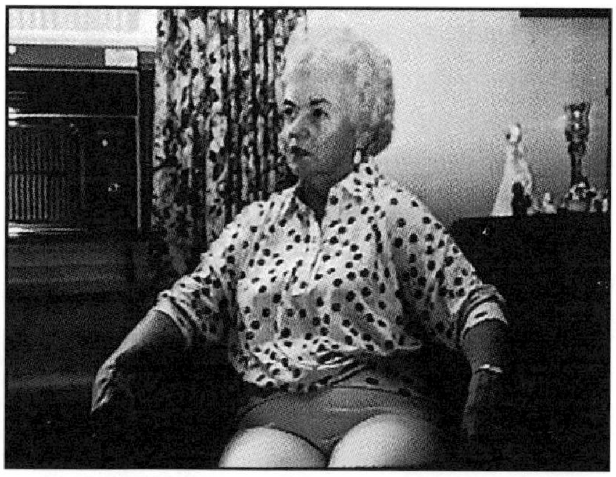

Above: Eleanor Boyle as she appeared on a video entitled, *The Work We've Done: The Contributions of Connecticut's Older Citizens to the Economy of the Nutmeg State.* It was co-produced in 1991 by the Connecticut State Department on Aging and the Urban League of Greater Hartford. Below: Eleanor working as a stenographer at Travelers, replete with earphones, during the 1940s.

Travelers Insurance Company

EB: I graduated from Stafford Springs high school. Inasmuch as we were still in the Depression, I just couldn't land a job at the Travelers, or any other company. My maiden aunt, with whom I lived, sent me to Morse Business College so I wouldn't get rusty with my typing and shorthand. I went to Morse all summer, with a few weeks off over Labor Day. Finally, the Travelers invited me to come in to discuss my application for employment. I left Morse at the end of October, and started in the Travelers November 1, 1938. Of course, the teachers at Morse did not want me to leave, as I had not yet earned my certificate. I told them I had to go, certificate or not, as I needed a job. I used to cry when I'd see other young people on the bus going to work and I didn't have a job. It was a difficult time. My mother and father had passed away, and I lived with my aunt in East Hartford. She was very anxious that I get into Travelers. In fact, she had to take me around to show me where the different insurance companies were, because I didn't know my way around Hartford.

TW: So, your first few years that you worked at Travelers, did you live with your aunt?

EB: Yes, my mother's sister.

TW: When you first went into the company, you joined the Steno department.

EB: I was placed in the stenographic pool.

TW: What did you do?

EB: I was an ediphone operator. The dictators used cylinders to record their dictation. I had to wear earphones all day. The cylinders were brought to the stenographic pool by runners. The clerk who handled the distribution had a board, similar to the board used in theaters to sell tickets, and as each clerk came up, she was handed a cylinder and a folder with files to help with the transcription. She recorded the time you took the cylinder and the time it was returned. She also measured the lines that you had typed with a cardboard ruler. This clerk kept track of your production for the supervisor. I always worried about my production, but apparently it was all right because I was never called to the supervisor's desk to discuss it. When you had a had to review the files in order to decipher what he was saying.

good dictator, it was fine, but when you got a poor dictator you After about two and a half years in the steno pool, I was allowed to go to the dictator's desk to take his dictation. You would go back to the pool, transcribe the dictation, deliver it to the dictator, return to the pool and go back on the ediphone.

I started at fourteen dollars per week, and that wasn't take home pay. My maiden aunt said to me one day, " I think you should ask for a raise." "Oh," I said, "no, they don't do that, you don't ask for raises, oh no!" She said, "Well, if you're not making very much money, you just simply tell your supervisor that you're sorry you can't live on what you are making." Well, I thought about it, and one day I got my courage up—I don't know how to this day. We would receive a two-dollar raise every year, if we were lucky. So, finally, I went to the supervisor and said, "I really think I have to have a raise, as I can't get along on what I'm making." She looked at me, and I continued adding, "I'd like it in my next pay, please." As I went on, I got more courage. I was given a four dollar raise in my next paycheck. My anniversary of employment was November, and normally your raise would be given late November or early December. The supervisor called me and said "They didn't kill your two dollar raise." I therefore received four dollars plus two dollars that year. I was in clover, but the pay was still very poor.

TW: Why would you be able to go to somebody and take dictation, rather than have him do it, rather than have him do it over the—

EB: Only certain dictators (depending on their titles) were allowed to have a stenographer. The dictator would call the Supervisor for a stenographer. If they liked your work, they would ask for you again. However, many would simply ask for any stenographer available.

After two years of taking dictation as a stenographer and transcribing from cylinders when you didn't have dictation, I was given the opportunity to try for the position of secretary to one of the officers in the group department. This officer's secretary left and he called the supervisor for a stenographer. She told me that he had lost his secretary and would be observing me as a possible replacement for his secretary. This was the way he always chose a secretary. Needless to say, I was very nervous. I passed inspection and was now a secretary to one of the officers in the group department.

The stenographic pool was all women. No men in those days. There was one chief supervisor and she had several units under her supervision. Each unit had a supervisor. I was in the group department steno pool. The ediphone operator and stenographers sat on one side of the room and the typists on the other side.

TW: If you were a typist, you weren't typing from the—

EB: No, if you were a typist, you just typed copy or set up charts. But as an ediphone operator, you transcribed, with your earphones on. It was very tedious at times.

TW: Do you remember how big the room was that you sat in?

EB: It was a very large room. I would guess the ediphone side had thirty or forty people and the typists about fifty.

The stenographic pool was all women. No men in those days. There was one chief supervisor and she had several units under her supervision. Each unit had a supervisor. I was in the group department steno pool. The ediphone operator and stenographers sat on one side of the room and the typists on the other side.

TW: How long did you work at Travelers?

EB: Forty-seven and a half years. I retired on May 1, 1986.

TW: You saw a lot of changes in the company.

EB: Oh yes, I saw many changes. I went from the stenographic pool to being a private secretary.

TW: How long were you a private secretary?

EB: About eight years. Then the man I worked for retired, and I went to work for another officer, and then they invited me back in 1950 to the stenographic department, in an administrative position. I was made an administrative assistant. The chief supervisor, Louise Reheiser, was the first woman officer at the Travelers. She had an assistant, and I was brought in as an understudy.

In 1959 the head of the department invited me to go the purchasing division, which was the first time they ever gave a woman an opportunity to be a buyer. He said, "I want you to go home and think about it, sleep on it." I said "I don't have to go home and sleep on it, I'll take it." He said, "You still go home and sleep on it, and discuss it with whoever you please." Well, I was back early in the morning to accept the position.

I went to the purchasing division with the title of purchasing assistant, which title they used instead of buyer. I knew absolutely nothing about buying. The men in the division did not want a woman in that capacity. They accepted me as a person because they all knew me, but as an equal—no way. Consequently, they did not help me. My friend who was secretary to the purchasing agent (we also lived together), and another friend who was secretary to the man who put me in the purchasing division, helped me. They would type my orders and explain various procedures. They knew that the men were trying to defeat me so I would give up.

I plugged along, for I was determined to succeed. It was a very interesting and challenging job. Finally came my big move to assistant purchasing agent. I was summoned to the office of the gentleman who had put me in the purchasing division. When I arrived, my immediate supervisor, the purchasing agent, was in his office. I thought, "What have I done wrong?" I was extremely nervous. But that day I was told that I was being promoted to assistant purchasing agent, effective January 1, 1966.

TW: Was that an officer's position?

EB: No. Many people in the Travelers thought I was an officer, but they never made me an officer. That was not an officer's position. Purchasing agent was an officer position. One of the men with the same title I had was also promoted to assistant purchasing agent, effective the same day. Now, he had only been there a short while, and I had been there seven years.

They played it up in the papers—first woman given an opportunity to be a buyer in the Travelers. I worked hard at it, because they were not helping me. I learned so much from the salespeople. They knew I was young, and I'd had no experience, so they would go out of their way to explain things to me. I mastered it. When the head of the stenographic division interviewed me, he said, "I think you have a very inquisitive mind, and I think you'll do just fine." And he says, "I really want to put a woman in there." And he really wasn't for pushing women. He put me in there, and then I had to make it on my own. I finally went up to him and said that I wasn't getting any cooperation, and I was trying very hard. "Well," he said, "men are running this company, and they will continue to run this company." I felt bad, because I wasn't saying that I want to be the chief honcho, I just want a little cooperation. So, I think he must have said something to the men, even though he wouldn't let me think he did. They sort of calmed down a little bit—not completely. But I always had the feeling that I had to work much harder at it than they did. They were watching all the time, hoping I'd stub my toe. But I guess they eventually respected me. And as I said, when the older men went, and the younger people came in, they accepted you, because that's the training they had.

TW: Were there ever any women that came in that you could help out?

EB: They brought in women as secretaries. They would help you and, of course, you would help them. And I had one girl I trained to be my assistant. I never withheld anything. I'd share my contacts with her, and my experiences. If I wasn't there, I knew that she could carry on, because I always felt, shame on me if I'm not in and she can't carry on. She was good—oh, she was excellent. She was bright, attractive, and was a very fast worker, and the salespeople liked her. She was a natural, and I was very proud, and we worked as a team beautifully. But she wasn't getting anywhere, and she finally posted out of the department. She is doing very well in her new department.

They gradually placed women into different jobs. Some of them had experience— some didn't. I look back, and think of all I gave to the company, and they didn't make me an officer. Now they push women right along. So, times have changed. Of course, time ran out on me. When I told my boss I was going to retire, he said, "You're going to retire? I thought you were going to stay until you were 70." I said, "Well, I've worked here over 47 years, I'm in good health, and I think it's time I left and played a little."

XII

Gladys Tantaquidgeon

Several interviews in this section have revealed the difficulties faced by female ethnic minorities in Connecticut, over the years. Gladys Tantaquidgeon, a Mohegan Native American, was born in New London, Connecticut at the end of the 19th century. At the time of writing, she is still overseeing and curating the Mohegan Museum in Montville, Connecticut. Like Laura Knott Twine, she overcame economic and social disadvantages, to record the experiences of her people. However, she had experienced much more, before becoming involved in the Mohegan Museum. She recounted those experiences to Tom Beardsley on June 6, 1994.

My name is Gladys Iola Tantaquidgeon. I was born in New London on June 15, 1899, so I'll soon be 95 years old. My parents then moved back to Montville, but returned to New London when I was old enough to start school because they did not like the school system in the Mohegan settlement in Montville. Nevertheless, I had a good start because I had taken lessons with my grandmother, so when I first started school, I didn't have to go into kindergarten, I went straight into the third grade at the Robert Bartlett school in New London.

So you could say I was the last of the Mohegans.

As a child, I remember the Mohegans celebrating the Green Corn Harvest during the last week in August. The tribal members held a Thanksgiving for the corn harvest. We have homecoming now, at the same time of the year. Nowadays, we don't have enough men living nearby to build a brush arbor and central to the celebration. A brush arbor is the New England equivalent to a tepee, but it is made from young saplings and covered with brush. The Mohegans had believed in the one great Spirit, and everything in nature was the work of that great Spirit, with the help of at least 37 lesser spirits.

I was brought up in the Christian faith, but we still preserve some of the old beliefs. I am a Congregationalist, and attend the Mohegan Congregational Church in Montville. Christianity played a large part in my life as I grew up, the entire family attended church. I went to Sunday School as a child. It was very strict. You had to be very quiet in church. I remember one day at church, my cousin and I, we had barely exchanged glances, but we got into trouble from the minister.

My mother was one of eight children, and her family were farmers and fishermen. My father just had one sister. The Mohegans, including my father's family, the Tantaquidgeons, and my mother's family, the Fieldings, originally occupied a large area between Norwich and New London.

My parents rented a house in Vauxhall street in New London, on the edge of town, close to the Perry Ice Ponds. My father worked for that company as an ice-cutter. As kids, we watched all the work that went on at the ice ponds. In those days, the sawing of the ice was all done by hand, and was stored in big ice houses. New London was a busy town. I remember the trolley cars, but we rarely used them, we mostly walked to school and to downtown. Way back, New London was a whaling town and some Mohegans worked as whalers. My father was a also self-taught carpenter.

We moved back to Montville when I was young. I remember that my father walked 9 miles into New London to work as a carpenter. We lived on what was left of the old Mohegan reservation in Montville, and I remember that my father supplemented the family income by doing a lot of hunting and fishing in this area, and lived through trading and barter. There was a good community atmosphere amongst the Mohegans that remained in the area. The Shantock state park was once part of the reservation, but we still use it as a burial ground for the tribe.

My mother did not work, she had a lot to do looking after the family. She tended to the woodstoves, made all the clothes for the children and cooked the food. My mother also helped relatives and friends. One of my mother's older sisters took care of the sick, with herbal medicines, so we looked after her.

I didn't go to High School, I left Connecticut in my early teens to go to Pennsylvania with Frank Speck, the head of the department of anthropology at the University of Pennsylvania. My family and the Specks had been friends for years. The Specks had a summer home nearby, and Frank and my older brother became friends. At that time, Frank was studying at Columbia, and working with my great aunt, Fedelia Fielding, who was the last living speaker of the Mohegan language. And that's how the family became acquainted with the Specks. Over the next six years I did research and took courses in American anthropology at the University of Pennsylvania. After that I got a position in the Heye Museum in New York. I don't know what they call it today.

I was working at the Museum one day, and I was told that Commissioner Collier, of the Bureau of Indian Affairs, wanted to see me. I thought, "what have I done now?" So I had to go to Washington, DC, to see him. He told me that they wanted to hire a community worker for the Yankton Sioux in South Dakota, so I went out there in the early 1920s, working for the Bureau on the reservation. I was like a social worker, and did a little bit of everything. A few years after that I was asked if I'd be interested in joining the Federal Arts and Crafts Board in Washington DC. I worked there for a while, and then was transferred to Rapid City, South Dakota, working on the Sioux reservation, helping out with arts and crafts, helping the older tribal members pass on their skills to the younger people, and helping them to get materials.

I retired out there, and then came home to Mohegan, Connecticut, and worked with my brother, Harold—a honorary tribal chief, in the Museum, which he opened here in 1931. I helped with tour groups and school classes, and a few years ago I wrote a paper about the Mohegan tradition of medicinal uses of herbs and plants. A lot of this knowledge was passed on to me from my grandmother, Lydia Fielding.

The Mohegans are part of the Delaware nation, and came to this section of Connecticut sometime during the 16th century from the upstate New York area, and were referred to as the "Pequotaug invaders." I think there are only 35 to 40 remaining Mohegan descendants in this area—the area which was home to Uncas, the famous Mohegan chief, in the 17th century. The word "Mohegan", means "wolf people." My name, "Tantaquidgeon," means running along fastly." Tantaquidgeon is the last surviving Mohegan name, so you could say I was the last of the Mohegans.

The Mohegan Museum (860-848-9145) is located on Route 32 in Montville. It is open Tuesday through Saturday, 10 a.m. until 3 p.m.

Tom Beardsley

Connecticut State Library

Above, left: Gladys Tantaquidgeon, the "Last of the Mohegans," poses among the artifacts on display in the Mohegan Museum in Montville, Connecticut. The Museum was founded in 1931 by Gladys and her late brother, Harold. Above, right: Gladys and Harold Tantaquidgeon pose in full Mohegan ceremonial dress, c. 1950. Note that the regalia Gladys is wearing is the one on display in the Mohegan Museum.

Select Bibliography

Suggestions for Further Reading

Alvarez, R. A., Kline, S. C., and McCutcheon, P. B., 1978. *Exploring Local History: Self Discovery Through the Humanities.* Washington, D.C., National Council on the Aging and the National Endowment for the Humanities.

Anker, L., 1993. "Immigrant Voices from the Federal Writers Project: The Connecticut Ethnic Survey, 1937-1940," in Gilbert, J., Gilman, A., Scott, D. M., and Scott, J. W., eds. *The Mythmaking Frame of Mind.* Belmont, CA: Wadsworth Publishing Company, 270-302.

Asher, R., 1983. *Connecticut Workers and Technological Change.* Storrs, CT: Center for Oral History, University of Connecticut.

Beardsley, T. R., 1990. *Willimantic Women: Their Lives & Labors.* Willimantic, CT: Windham Textile & History Museum.

_______1993. *Willimantic Industry & Community: The Rise & Decline of a Connecticut Textile City. Willimantic,* CT: Windham Textile & History Museum.

Boydston, J., Kelley, M., and Margolis, A., eds. 1988. *The Limits of Sisterhood: The Beecher Sisters on Women's Rights and Woman's Sphere.* Chapel Hill: University of North Carolina Press.

Brecher, J., Lombardi, J., and Stackhouse, J., eds. 1982. *Brass Valley: The Story of Working Peoples' Lives and Struggles in an American Industrial Region.* Philadelphia, Temple Univ. Press.

______1986. *How to Uncover and Tell the Story of Your Community, Association or Union.* New Haven, CT: Commonwork Pamphlets/Advocate Press.

Brusic, L. M., 1986. *Amidst Cultivated and Pleasant Fields: A Bicentennial History of North Haven, Connecticut.* North Haven Historical Society.

Bucki, C., 1980. *Metal, Minds & Machines: Waterbury at Work.* Mattatuck Historical Society.

Buel, J. D., and R., 1984. *The Way of Duty: A Woman and Her Family in Revolutionary America.* New York: W. W. Norton.

Carlson, R. G., ed. 1987. *Rooted Like the Ash Trees: New England Indians & the Land.* Naugatuck, CT: Eagle Wing Press.

Clouette, B. A., 1984. *Bristol, Connecticut: A Bicentennial History, 1785-1985.* Bristol Public Library & Phoenix Publications.

______1987. *Immigrants: Connecticut's Diverse Ethnic Heritage.* Connecticut Centennial Commission for the Statue of Liberty and Ellis Island.

______1992. "Getting Their Share: Irish and Italian Immigrants in Hartford, Connecticut, 1850-1940." Ph.D. dissertation, University of Connecticut (Storrs).

Collier, C., & B., 1983. *The Connecticut Scholar (No. 6): The Literature of Connecticut History.* Middletown, CT: Connecticut Humanities Council.

Dart, M. S., 1965. *Yankee Traders At Sea and Shore.* New York: William Frederick Press.

Dunaway, D. K., and Baum, W. K., eds., 1984. *Oral History: An Interdisciplinary Anthology.* Nashville, Tennessee: American Association for State & Local History.

Erikson, C., 1990 reprint. *Invisible Immigrants: The Adaptation of English and Scottish Immigrants in Nineteenth-century America.* Cornell University Press.

Grele, R. J., 1991. *Envelopes of Sound: The Art of Oral History.* Westport, CT: Praeger.

Guthman, W. H., 1980. *The Correspondence of Captain Nathan and Lois Peters, April 25, 1775—February 5, 1777.* Hartford: The Connecticut Historical Society.

Gutman, H., and Bell, D. H., eds. 1987. *The New England Working Class and the New Labor History.* Urbana: University of Illinois Press.

Houseley, K. L., 1993. *The Letter Kills But the Spirit Gives Life: The Smiths: Abolitionists, Suffragists, Bible Translators.* Historical Society of Glastonbury.

Kline, P. C., 1939. "New Light on the Yankee Peddler," *New England Quarterly,* 12:1, 80-98.

Lewis, T. R., 1976 . "Silk Along Steel: The Story of the South Manchester Railroad." (Chester, CT)

Moynihan, R. B., 1988. "Coming of Age: Four Centuries of Connecticut Women and Their Choices." *The Connecticut Historical Society Bulletin.* Volume 53, Nos 1 & 2, Winter/Spring.

_______Russett, C., and Crumpacker, L., eds. 1993 (Two Volumes). *Second to None: A Documentary History of American Women.* University of Nebraska Press.

Nichols, C., 1983. *Votes and More for Women: Suffrage and After in Connecticut.* New York: Institute for Research in History and Haworth Press.

Pennybacker, S. D., 1995. "East Side Story," *Hartford Courant,* July 2, 1995.

Roth, D. M., and Grenier, J. A., eds. 1985. *Connecticut History & Culture: An Historical Overview and Resource Guide for Teachers.* Hartford, CT: The Connecticut Historical Commission and the Center for Connecticut Studies at Eastern Connecticut State University.

Schwartz, L. A., 1983. "Immigrant Voices in Home, Work, and Community: Women and Family in the Migration Process, 1890-1930." Ph.D. dissertation, SUNY (Stony Brook).

Shuldiner, D., 1995. *Aging Political Activists: Personal Narratives From the Old Left.* Westport, CT: Praeger.

Simmons, W. S., 1984. *The Spirit of the New England Tribes: Indian History & Folklore,* 1620-1984. Hanover, New Hampshire: University Press of New England.

Smith, C. C., (Chief Big Eagle of Pequannock tribe, Paugussett nation, Trumbull, CT) 1985. *Quarter-Acre of Heartache.* Blacksburg, VA: Pochahontas Press.

Stave, B. M., 1979. "Making Hartford Home: An Oral History of Twentieth Century Ethnic Development in Connecticut's Capital City," in Sondra A. Stave, ed., *Hartford: The City and the Region, Past, Present, Future.* Hartford.

______and Sutherland, J. F., eds. 1985. *Talking About Connecticut: Oral History in the Nutmeg State.* np.

______and Palmer, M. 1991. *Mills & Meadows: A Pictorial History of Northeast Connecticut.* Virginia Beach, VA: The Donning Company.

______and Sutherland, J. F., with Salerno, A. 1994. *From The Old Country: An Oral History of European Migration to America.* New York: Twayne Publishers.

Strotter, H. T., 1962. *The Underground Railroad in Connecticut. Middletown,* CT: Wesleyan University.

Tantaquidgeon, G., 1972. "Plants and Plant Uses of the Mohegan of Connecticut," in *Folk Medicine of the Delaware and Related Algonkian Indians.* Harrisburg, PA: The Pennsylvania Historical and Museum Commission's Anthropological Series, No. 3.

Thompson, Paul., 1978. *The Voice of the Past: Oral History.* Oxford University Press.

Townshend, C. H., 1900. "The Quinnipiack Indians and Their Reservation," in *Papers of the New Haven Historical Society,* Vol. VI, 151-219.

Wyllys Papers, The., 1924. "Correspondence and Documents Chiefly of Descendants of Governor George Wyllys of Connecticut, 1590-1796." Hartford: Connecticut Historical Society.

Connecticut Humanities Council